MODELLING World War I Trench Warfare

BRITISH FRONT LINE DUGOUT
Basic Shelter for Officers

MODELLING World War I Trench Warfare

Andy Belsey

THE CROWOOD PRESS

First published in 2021 by
The Crowood Press Ltd
Ramsbury, Marlborough
Wiltshire SN8 2HR

enquiries@crowood.com

www.crowood.com

British Library Cataloguing-in-Publication Data
A catalogue record for this book is available from the British Library.

ISBN 978 1 78500 858 0

Typeset by Simon and Sons
Cover design by Blue Sunflower Creative
Printed and bound in India by Parksons Graphics Pvt. Ltd., Mumbai.

Contents

Acknowledgements and Dedication

The author wishes to thank the following for their help:

Adrian Bay, Pete and Tansy Belsey, Sue Belsey, Sam and Mel Belsey, John Bones, Mike Butler, Toby and Richard Dingle, Craig Hedgecock, Paul Marshall, Simon Parfitt, Darren Parker-Mead, Bryan Parry, Andy Robertshaw, Oliver and Sarah Taylor, William Wood, 10th Essex Living History Group, Memorial Museum Passchendaele 1917, Lee Atkins and Kevin Mullane of 3DD Models.

This book is dedicated to my grandfathers, Gunner Ernest Belsey and Corporal Herbert Sanders, who survived the Great War.

Gunner Ernest Belsey, RGA.

Corporal Herbert Sanders, Essex Yeomanry.

Introduction

The author with his ten trench sections.

I did not originally intend to make a series of section models, but one model led to another as I thought of a sphere of trench warfare that I had not tackled before. My models are visual explanations of World War I trenches and I have considered carefully what to include within parameters that were set when building my first section model. These educational models can show visually what would take many words to explain. The miniature world has a fascination for many of us and modelmaking is a craft that gives great pleasure to lots of people. I am a modelmaker who enjoys history.

I have gathered information about trench warfare from many sources, processing the most important details, and can now consolidate most of that in this one book. I am a perfectionist when it comes to representing details correctly, which means that I try to refine and improve my work wherever possible. Any mistakes in my models bother me terribly, but perfectionism is a blessing and a curse.

I have learnt much from other modelmakers, but I have tried to find easy techniques of my own that should be straightforward to copy. I used to blog about the construction of my models on the Military Modelling Forum until it ceased operations in early 2018. The worldwide attention that my models gained inspired my own website (https://andybelseymodels.wixsite.com), and I continue to blog about their construction on the Scale Models Forum and planetFigure. The beauty of the internet is that it connects those with similar passions and I have recently teamed up with Mike (the Kiwi) Butler in New Zealand. I can create intricate detail and sculpt, but Mike has an extraordinary ability with paint and you will find that he has painted and enhanced several figures in this book. Our skill sets combine to the best advantage, and we have fun together while we do it.

My own interest in the Great War started with how it affected my grandparents and their siblings. I inherited a large collection of family memorabilia (mainly paperwork) from World War I and have spent years researching how my family were involved. They were mainly farm workers and some were Methodists who didn't want to kill but were prepared to help with medical tasks. One was gassed and another shot in the leg while recovering the wounded, so it was not a safe job. Two great uncles and a cousin were killed by the conflict. My paternal grandfather, Ernest Belsey, had emigrated to Canada in 1905 and had Canadian citizenship by the time war started. The plan was for his younger brother Bert to join him but, as the war progressed, they realized that it was only a matter of time before Bert would be

Mike Butler's amazing painting of my converted Tommy's War figure. A 54mm figure with hairy arms and veins on his hands!

conscripted. Ernest returned to Kent in 1916 and they volunteered, enlisting with the Royal Garrison Artillery in the hope that they could stay together. Because of the devastation on small communities caused by the Somme battles of 1916, the brothers were not allowed to be in the same gun team, but were both able to join the 108th Heavy Battery in Belgium. Just before Ernest went to war, he met my grandmother, Alice Bones, in England. They only met because of the Great War, so my existence is a consequence of the war.

I started modelling Great War trenches in 2006 by helping my friend Chris Yelf with a model for Newhaven Fort in Sussex, which commemorated the 90th anniversary of the Battle of the Somme. It was difficult then to find basic information with dimensions. After completing that model I resolved to make a more detailed trench model of my own, without the constraints of commercial

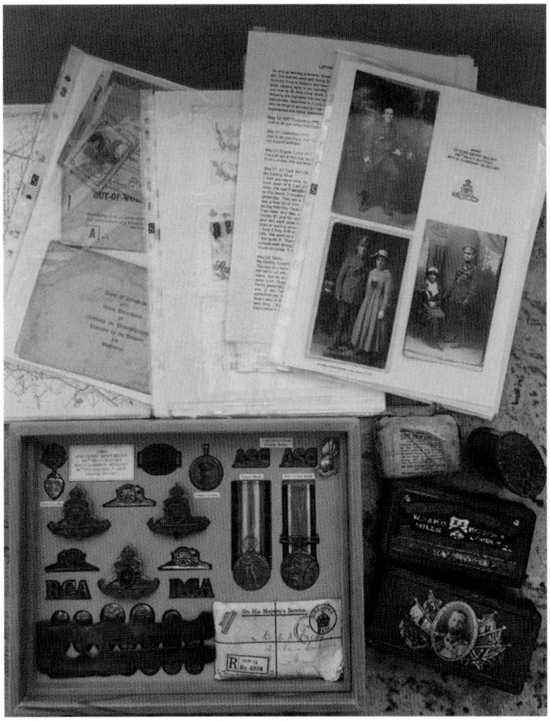

Part of my family's memorabilia. Under the photos are papers explaining my grandfather's war service and documents such as his Discharge Papers. I have ten history trays like this.

modelmaking. The result was my 1:285 scale diorama of Somme front line trenches, which features in the next chapter.

THE GREAT WAR (A FUTILE WAR?)

My models concentrate on the Western Front, the main theatre where World War I would be lost or won. As nobody knew that another world war might follow, this first global conflict was referred to as the 'Great War'. In recent years we have been fed a story of it being a wasteful, futile war that went nowhere and achieved nothing. Brave soldiers were vainly sent to their deaths in thousands by daft old generals who stayed miles behind the front, away from danger and out of touch. This very simplistic view, however, was not held by most of those who fought in it. The Allied high command were slower to adapt and guilty of stubbornly pursuing impossible targets, whereas the Germans encouraged reports from those on the actual battlefield and their evolving response enabled them to continually baffle Allied attacks.

Tactics were adapted and lessons were learnt by both sides. As the war went on, although the band of defence grew to miles rather than yards, it came to depend more upon strong points, built around machine gun positions, which supported each other. Continuous trench lines were much easier to target, so the manned positions were disguised as much as possible, with many of the troops emerging from underground shelters only when defence was necessary.

Although the battles were fought over a narrow swathe of France and Belgium for just over four years, there were great advances in technology during and as a result of the war. One of the greatest of these was the tank, which could ride over barbed wire and trenches, but development was needed to bring them to their full potential. There were also huge developments in aeroplanes: the frail machines of 1914 bore little resemblance to the robust aeroplanes of 1918. Other significant wartime developments were portable machine guns, trench mortars, radio, gas, attack submarines, aircraft carriers and plastic surgery.

The battles of 1918 were fought with close cooperation between the services. Rather than days of bombardment before an assault, which warned the defender exactly where an attack was coming, the barrage would be short but heavy, to keep the defence in their shelters. Creeping barrages were developed where the artillery would gradually move the area of bombardment forward, with troops following behind as closely as possible to overwhelm the defence before it had time to recover from the shelling and emerge from the shelters they had been forced into. Aeroplanes would fly overhead, feeding back to their commanders as much information as they could about progress so that plans could be adapted.

The British involvement and casualties of the war cannot be looked at in isolation. The Somme battles were necessary to draw German attention away from Verdun, where the French were struggling. The slaughter of so many British and Commonwealth soldiers in a tiny area around Ypres happened because it was of huge political and strategic value, being the last corner of unoccupied Belgium, for whom Britain had entered the war. The area also sheltered the route to the Channel ports, through which most supplies came.

British propaganda constantly tried to portray the Germans as barbaric monsters and yet the Christmas truces showed the common soldier that there was little difference between the ordinary people of the opposing nations apart from their conflicting ambitions. The Allied Victory Medals label the war as 'The Great War for Civilisation' and the term 'Hun' was used to link the Germans to one of the barbarian tribes who destroyed Roman civilization. Today the British are still quick to point out that the Germans started the war by invading tiny Belgium and were first to use terrible weapons like gas, flamethrowers, mines and submarines. They attempted to keep the moral high ground by claiming the British just retaliated, but they widely used and refined the use of all these tools. Little is spoken about how the German population was starved by the naval blockade. History is always written by the victor, who selects which story is told and what is overlooked. War is cruel and my wish is to educate rather than promote war. History repeats itself because people do not listen or learn from it.

MUDDY TRENCHES

Our typical image of the Great War is of waterlogged, muddy trenches, which dominated the battlefields. Trenches had been used for centuries but never on the scale that soon developed in 1914. As the war progressed, the bands of defence stretched back several miles behind the actual 'front line'. The industrialization of Europe had brought a new generation of more powerful and accurate weapons and the military commanders were not prepared for the type of siege warfare that soon developed in the trenches. The main reason for digging trenches was for shelter against high explosive shells, fired by quick-firing artillery. Troops caught in the open were extremely vulnerable and needed to find shelter as soon as possible. The vast majority of casualties in the war (about 60 per cent) were caused by shelling, not machine guns. Once an area was entrenched and defended with barbed wire, machine guns

The 1:285 scale diorama in black and white. Most modern images of trenches show a mass of brown mud.

The same image in colour, showing how the battlefield was much more colourful than we imagine.

and field artillery, it was very difficult to dislodge the defender and any attempt would cause many casualties among the attacking force. Four and a quarter years were spent trying new techniques and weaponry to get through the enemy lines and break the deadlock of trench warfare. Trenches were actually a place of relative safety, rather than the hellholes we imagine.

Most of the coloured images of the trenches show a brown mass of muddy ground, with water-filled shell holes. This was not the usual battlefield for most of the war; if you study the black and white photographs more carefully, you will notice plenty of grass and vegetation, and anyone who has tended a garden will know how quickly weeds return. Therefore even when the ground was excavated, gassed or bombarded, it would soon have traces of green and colour from weeds.

THE BASICS OF CONSTRUCTING TRENCHES

The type of soil and its position, the weather, the amount of shelling on an area and what building materials were available would all affect the way that a trench was constructed. Any excavation would need supporting with revetment, to stop the walls from caving in due to gravity or weather taking its toll. Many materials could be used to do this and each country had its own preferences. I have attempted to show as diverse revetment as possible on my models to indicate how trenches could differ in appearance. Areas within the same trench line could vary as they were damaged through bombardment or repaired from the effects of age and weather. No two trenches would look exactly the same. Trenches would also change occupants, if they were captured, or when allies transferred parts of the line in redeployment. Therefore you could find British troops occupying a captured German-style trench with woven branches or Germans occupying a trench with 'A' frames and corrugated iron, which were typically British. Revetment was done with what was available, repaired with what could be found, and the results were usually far from ideal. Whatever the textbook said, on the battlefield, often under horrible conditions, men were usually just trying to survive and longing to be in the reserve lines as soon as possible. Soldiers worked half-heartedly to get the job done quickly in the hope of getting a little rest – after all, it might soon be destroyed.

Postcard showing preserved trenches at Dixmude, Belgium. The revetment incorporates sandbags, hurdles and timber.
BRYAN PARRY

Plate 40.

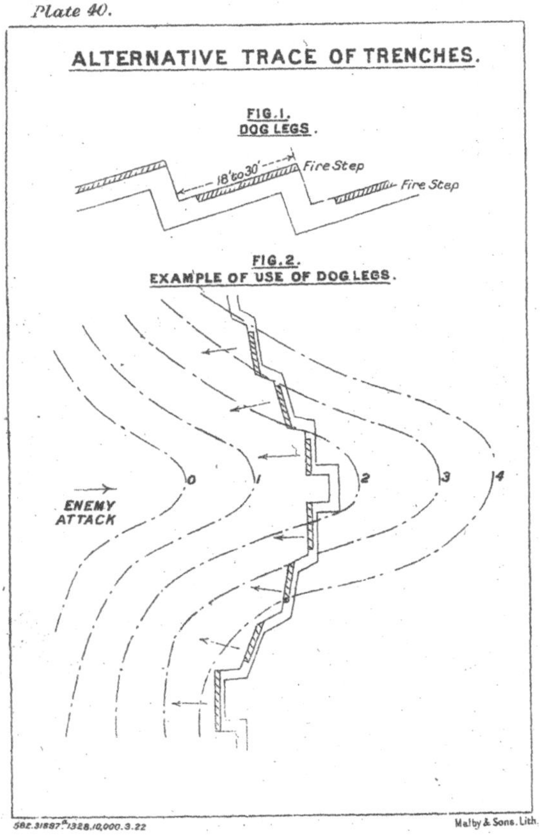

Plan showing how the topography of the land would affect the trench layout, from the Manual of Fieldworks (All Arms), *1921.*

Although there were instructions on how trenches should be constructed, building under battlefield conditions in the cold and dark, with the threat of shells or bullets, made construction very difficult in practice. Work and repairs to trenches was often done at night to avoid being shelled by the enemy, who would hamper any defence being made stronger. Chalk soil (typically found near the River Somme) is tougher to dig, but will drain rainwater well and is less likely to collapse. Clay soil is much more problematic because it needs much more support and collects rainwater, which cannot drain away. In some clay soil areas (especially in Flanders, Belgium) it was impossible to dig, as any excavation would immediately fill with water, so walls of soil were built up above ground level.

It was calculated that it would take about 40in (101cm) of normal soil to stop a bullet, whereas it could be stopped in chalk in 15in (38cm). Parapets in clay soil were ideally deeper, as it could take 80in (202cm) of clay to stop bullets.

Trenches were dug with traverse corners to give regular shelter from enfilade (gunfire from the side). A shell burst could be mostly contained within one of these short lengths called firebays, which would be between 18ft and 30ft

The construction of the revetment could vary depending on what was available (Tommy's War bases adapted by the author). Sandbags and timber revetment.

Chicken wire on a wooden frame.

Wicker hurdle revetment.

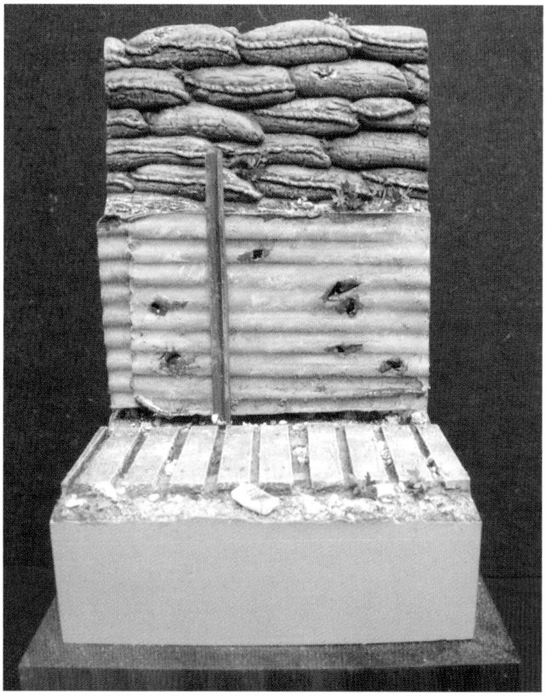

Sandbags and corrugated iron revetment.

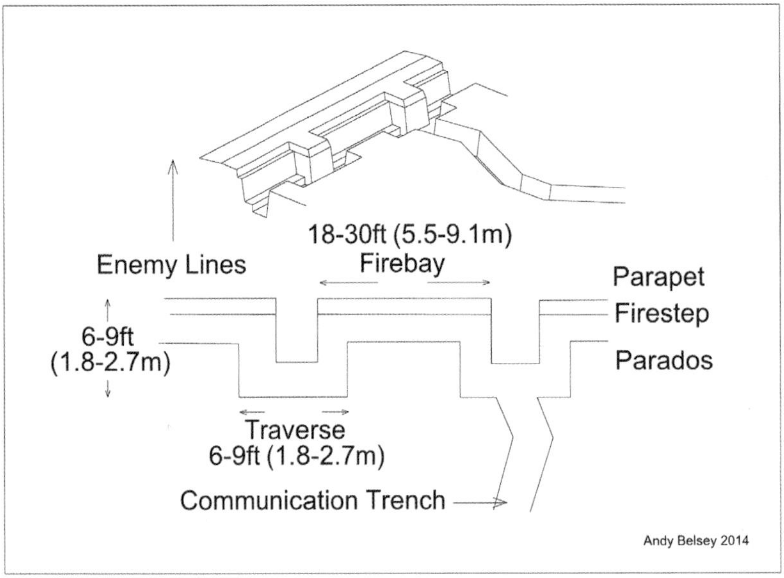

Plan showing dimensions of a basic firebay.

(5.5–9.7m) in length. At each end it would turn back about 6–9ft (1.8–2.7m), and then run parallel for about 9ft (2.7m) before turning forward into the next firebay.

Ideally trenches were dug to a depth of at least 5ft (1.5m) below ground to be deep enough to shelter a standing man's head. They were about 6ft 6in (2m) wide at ground level, narrowing to about 2ft (0.6m) at their base. Revetment was done as soon as possible to prevent the sides from collapsing and ideally the revetment would be further supported by tethered spikes, attached to the tops of the supporting posts, which would be buried under the soil heaps. Soil dug from the trench was piled in front and behind to increase their height up to about 9ft (2.7m).

About 2–3ft (0.6–0.9m) above the trench floor, facing the enemy, it would widen to form the 'firestep'. Standing on this higher shelf would allow the defender a view over the parapet from which he could fire his weapon to defend the position. Only during battle or at night would a soldier expose his head above the parapet or front soil pile, as snipers would watch for unsuspecting soldiers.

The floor of the trench was ideally lined with wooden duckboards and even raised off the floor to give a 'sump' space underneath, into which rainwater could drain to keep the soldiers' feet dry.

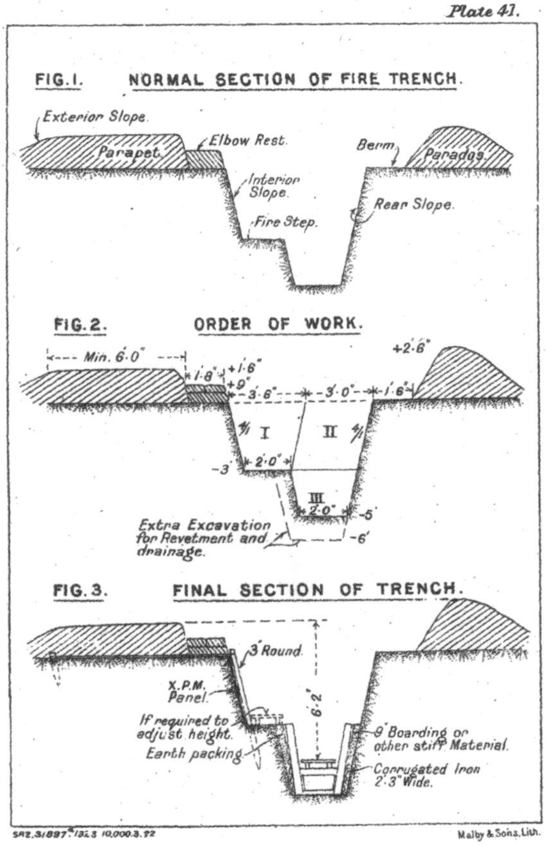

Engineer's drawings of how a trench should be constructed, from the War Office's Manual of Fieldworks (All Arms), *1921.*

THE MODELS

The small-scale diorama led on to creating ten section models, which describe differing aspects of Great War trenches from a mainly British perspective. Although they look similar at first glance, I have tried to include varying details in each to show national preferences and different types of revetment, as well as extra features about life in the trenches. Each section is labelled to point to the main aspects. I chose 1:32 scale so that I could use the figures by Tommy's War, which I considered the best on the market. I then met the company's owner, Darren Parker-Mead, and now find myself making bases for him using the knowledge gained creating my own models.

The models were popular exhibits at the 'Remembering 1916' exhibition held at Whitgift School in South London during 2016–17. I am proud to have been part of a much acclaimed exhibition that attracted more than 35,000 visitors. I am often told that my models should be in a museum, but for now they educate viewers online worldwide and this book gives me the opportunity to further explain their content and context. Each model tells a different story.

The author with his models at the 'Remembering 1916' exhibition, Whitgift School, 2016–17.

British trench raiders in a German trench: Tommy's War diorama painted by Ernesto Reyes, using figures by Nino Pizzichemi on a base by the author. DARREN PARKER-MEAD

One of the dioramas at the 'Remembering 1916' exhibition.

Chapter One

British Front Line Trenches of the Somme, 1916: a 1:285 Scale Model

This model shows a small area of British front line trenches as they appeared on the battlefields of the Somme in 1916. You will immediately notice that the battlefield is still green and has remains of its previous life as farmland. Small roads run through it and the remnants of a farm may be

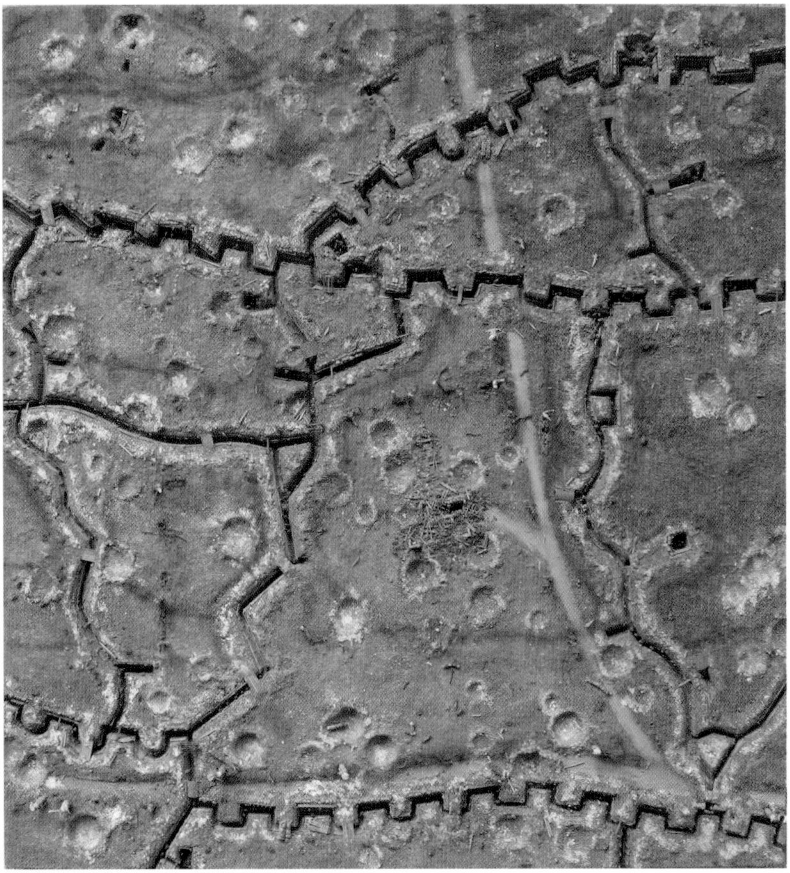

Plan view of the model. Trenches can be confusing.

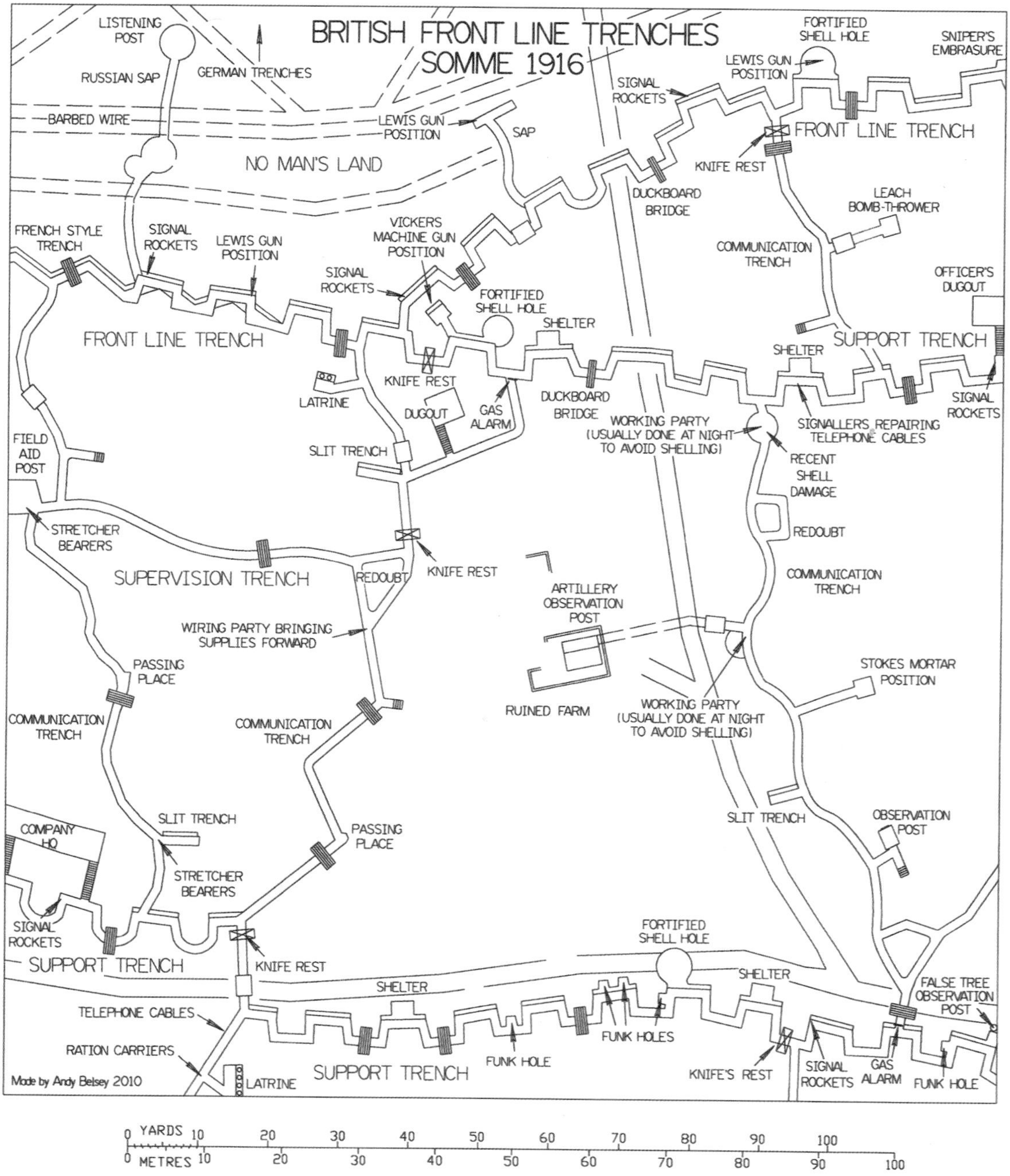

Labelled plan explaining the model's features.

seen among the shell-shattered trees. The Somme area was full of vegetation while the battle went on and the soldiers crossed no man's land covered by tall grass. An attempt has been made to include as much as possible from a typical area of the front in a zone of about 140 yards or 130m square, although it does not represent a specific part of the British lines.

TRENCH TYPES AND FEATURES

Trench Lines

The rows of trenches are purposely made a little confusing, and not completely parallel, because the actual trenches were often dug in apparently random ways, depending on the terrain or circumstances. Textbook trench diagrams usually show parallel rows of neat trenches, but this rarely happened on the battlefield. This model shows two lines of traversed trenches, but the front line has an extra spur running out closer towards the enemy lines. If it was felt that part of no man's land was too wide, then a spur would be dug closer to the enemy before he dominated that space. There is also an untraversed trench, called a 'supervision trench', running parallel, but just behind, part of the front line. This type of trench was used as a passageway to pass through quickly because it had no corners to negotiate. The secondary support line behind has been staggered either side of a communication trench.

Somme Chalk

The model shows chalky soil piles that make the trenches obvious. This was unavoidable as the Somme chalk was just under the surface and could not be hidden. The shadows of trench excavations were highlighted by the brightness of piled chalk, making aerial photography to mark trench positions very easy. Because we are used to seeing black and white images, the white of the chalk is only noticeable if it is pointed out.

Front line showing a Lewis gun team in the foreground. Chalk in the soil piles make the trenches very obvious.

No Man's Land

The area between the opposing forces, called 'no man's land', was usually several hundred yards wide but could be as narrow as 10 yards. Each side would place rows of barbed wire a few yards in front of their trench to stop the enemy getting too close, but some of it would be laid less densely to lure an attacker into areas covered by machine guns.

Support and Reserve Lines

About 70 to 200 yards (64m–183m) behind the front line there would be more traversed trenches. There could be as many as six lines of roughly parallel trenches called 'support' or 'reserve lines', dug up to 4 miles behind to give extra security. If trenches were captured then there would be a secondary line of defence to fall back to and from which a counter-attack could be launched as soon as possible, before the enemy had time to establish himself.

Communication Trenches

The traversed trenches, called 'lines', were connected by 'communication trenches', which meandered or zigzagged between the lines, giving a safe passage from one line to another. Again the corners were designed to hide a view along these trenches and to give some shelter to the troops using them. From the sides of communication trenches other passageways led to latrines, mortar pits, observation posts or short trenches from which to mount a defence. Some communication trenches were designated alternately 'up' or 'down' for one-way passage. If they were used as a two-way passage, then sporadic, wider passing places would be dug into the walls to enable those travelling in the opposite direction to pass. Sharp corners were always avoided to enable a stretcher to be carried along them.

Navigation

Trench lines and communication trenches were usually named and signposted to help troops navigate the maze of confusing passageways. They were often named by their original occupants, choosing names from their homelands, and you may notice one of these trenches is called 'Epsom Downs', which is near where I live. Communication trenches were often called 'avenues' with neighbouring ones named in alphabetical order to further aid navigation.

Saps

From the front line, out into no man's land and closer to the enemy, shallow trenches called 'saps' were dug, as a place for a light machine gun position or as a 'listening post' where soldiers would try to gain information about the enemy's movements. 'Russian saps' were dug as tunnels, so that troops could get much closer to the enemy without being seen. On the model is a short sap equipped with a Lewis gun coming from the spur and a longer Russian sap connecting shell holes, which eventually leads to a listening post where soldiers are on duty.

Machine Guns

You will notice machine gun emplacements, mortar pits and observation posts among the trenches. They are purposely not camouflaged on the model, but if they were as obvious as this in reality they would soon become targets to be shelled by the enemy. The optimum sighting of machine guns would have them firing obliquely across no man's land, so that the attacker would have to cross the paths of at least two guns, and areas of barbed wire would be laid less densely, to lure an attacker into killing zones where guns were sighted.

Dugouts

There are several dugouts on the model; some are on the sides of the model, enabling you to see into them. Small shelters were made for officers or as medical centres to treat light wounds. A small dugout, where a couple of officers could shelter, is exposed at the edge of the front line, and a larger Company HQ is on the edge of the reserve line. The ordinary ranks had to make do with less elaborate scrapes into trench walls called 'funk holes', or under sheets of curved corrugated iron called 'elephant iron'. The model has funk holes dug in

Vickers machine gun position with a knife rest obstacle nearby.

One of the dugouts revealed on the side of the model.

the walls of the support line. Dugouts and shelters were best placed in the front wall of a trench, as it was less likely that a shell would land in its entrance, as well as being hidden from enemy view.

Field Aid Post

On the edge of the supervision trench is a small shelter called a Field Aid Post (FAP), where a medical officer would be based. His job was to maintain the health of the men immediately around him. Light wounds could be treated by this officer, so that troops were back on duty as soon as possible. More serious wounds could be given basic care, to stabilize their condition, until they were given more extensive treatment further back, away from the front line. The model shows a soldier wounded

Casualty being carried into the Field Aid Post.

Latrine with ration carriers passing by through a communication trench.

from recent shelling being carried into the FAP on a stretcher for immediate treatment. A second pair of stretcher-bearers is further back down the communication trench, returning with an empty stretcher from an Advanced Dressing Station in the reserve lines. Each unit had non-combatants, assigned as stretcher-bearers, who would support their medical officer in the care of the fighting troops. On quiet days the officer would inspect the men's feet for signs of trench foot, caused by having wet feet for a prolonged period. It is a serious condition that can lead to gangrene and to the amputation of the foot.

Hygiene

There are two latrines on the model, dug from the sides of communication trenches. These were toilets with containers to urinate into or basic seats above soil pits for excrement. When these were full the area would be buried again and another dug nearby. They were unsafe, smelly places where the troops were unlikely to linger for too long. It was important to set places for sanitation to prevent disease or infection of wounds. The first hastily dug trenches of 1914 had no sanitation, so troops would squat over a spade and catapult their excrement into no man's land, but if shellfire landed on it, it could be thrown everywhere, potentially infecting wounds caused by the same explosion.

Air War

The war above the trenches is also shown on this model, although an aircraft is very unlikely to have crash-landed so close to front lines. The Fokker Eindecker monoplane will soon be salvaged for scrap and souvenirs taken. If the pilot has survived, he will be taken for interrogation. The Eindecker was a pioneering machine equipped with a forward-facing machine gun that fired between the propeller blades, thanks to an interrupter gear mechanism that allowed the pilot to aim his aeroplane and fire at the enemy he was flying towards. The Eindecker gave the Germans the command of the skies in early 1916 and the Allies' initial response was to build 'pusher' planes like the Airco DH.2. The backward-facing propellers gave the pilot the ability to fire forward, but the tail frame had to be built around the backward-facing engine. The DH.2 on the model flies low to get a closer look at the crashed Eindecker. The British soon discovered the secret of the mechanism and built it into their own aircraft.

This model does not show artillery, as even field artillery would be sited at least 750 yards (685m) from the front line. Separate models were created to show artillery (*see* Chapter 14).

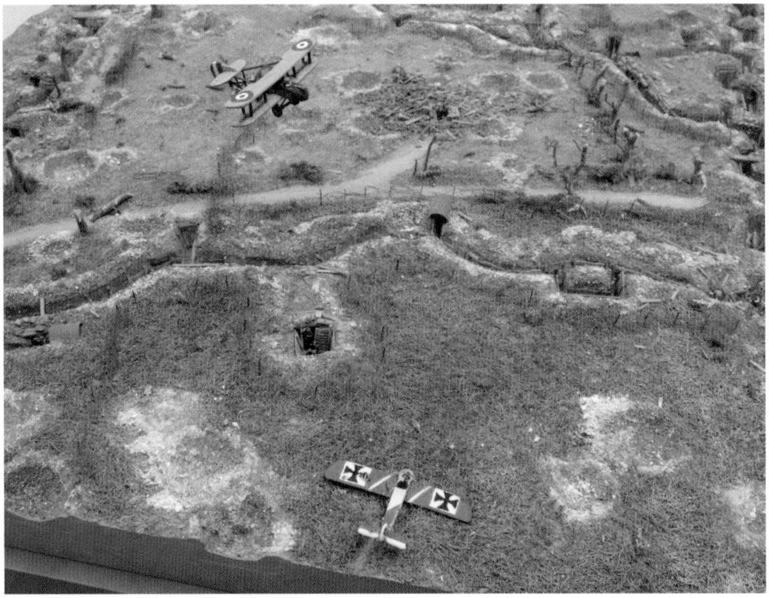

An Airco DH.2 flies low to take a look at the crashed Fokker Eindecker.

Scratch-built aeroplanes, carved in styrene.

CREATING THE DIORAMA MODEL

The plans for this model were drawn using CAD (computer aided drawing) and then the basic trenches cut into an 18mm MDF board with a computer numerical control (CNC) router. The parameters of the model were determined by the size of an acrylic case rescued from a redundant architectural model. The case was roughly 500mm square, giving an area of about 140 yards (130m) square at 1:285 scale to work within. By showing just a small portion of no man's land, there was room for two rows of trenches spaced about 93 yards (85m) apart.

Basic Groundwork

To avoid the terrain being flat, a Dremel with a drum sanding bit was used to grind undulations into the groundwork. Discs of three different sizes

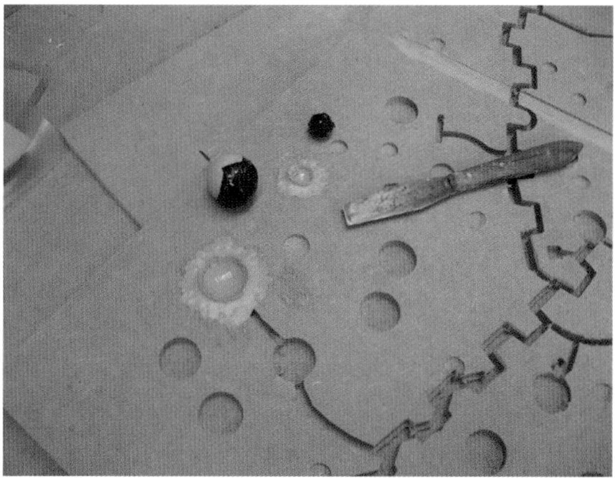

Making shell craters with car body filler in the CNC routed MDF board.

Revetting the trench walls, adding soil piles and sandbags.

were routed into the base with the CNC to create shell craters. Car body filler was pasted into these, and while it was wet a wooden ball, covered with adhesive tape as a release coating, was pressed in. When the filler was semi-dry and still a little soft, the ball was pulled out and the rim of the crater carved to soften its profile.

Revetment

The CNC router created vertical trench walls, but an incline was carved along every wall with a scalpel to widen and round the tops. Many hours were spent cladding the walls with a variety of materials. Wood was created with styrene using individual strips or wider pieces with grooves scribed into them. It was much quicker to clad with the larger scribed pieces, but using individual pieces results in more irregular and typically shabby-looking trenches. Metal foil from scalpel packets was used to recreate corrugated iron, which was then embossed with a fingernail over a ribbed surface. The 'corrugated' foil only required cutting into scale 6ft sheets. Chicken wire was made from fine nylon netting. After the walls were clad with this assortment of materials, vertical support posts were added, made of styrene strip. Duckboards were made by scribing 1mm spaced parallel lines into a sheet of 0.25mm styrene; 2mm strips were then cut in the opposite direction, producing ribbed strips. This was the simplest method of making the many lengths of duckboards needed.

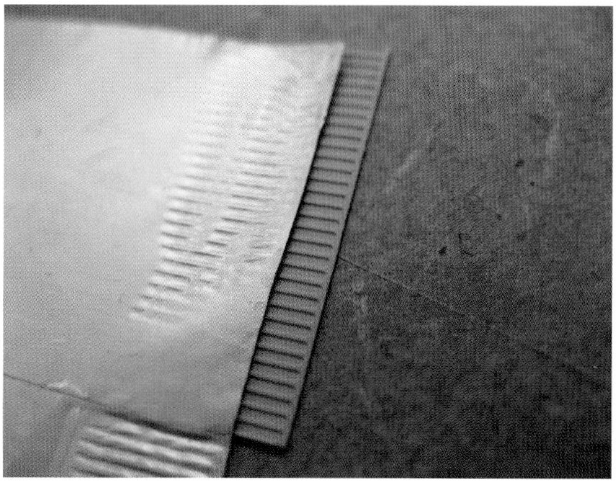

Embossing metal foil for corrugated iron.

Rows of sandbags were created by rolling 1.5mm sausages of Milliput epoxy putty, which were partially cut every couple of millimetres to create individual bags and then laid in rows on top of each other. Once a few lengths were created, silicone moulds were made to reduce the effort of creating hundreds of sandbags. Silicone moulds of dugout entrances (made from a mixture of styrene and Milliput) were also formed. The sandbag castings were stuck along the parapets before adding soil piles in Polyfilla and car body filler, which would be higher than the surrounding area. The car body filler was pasted on as the catalyst cured

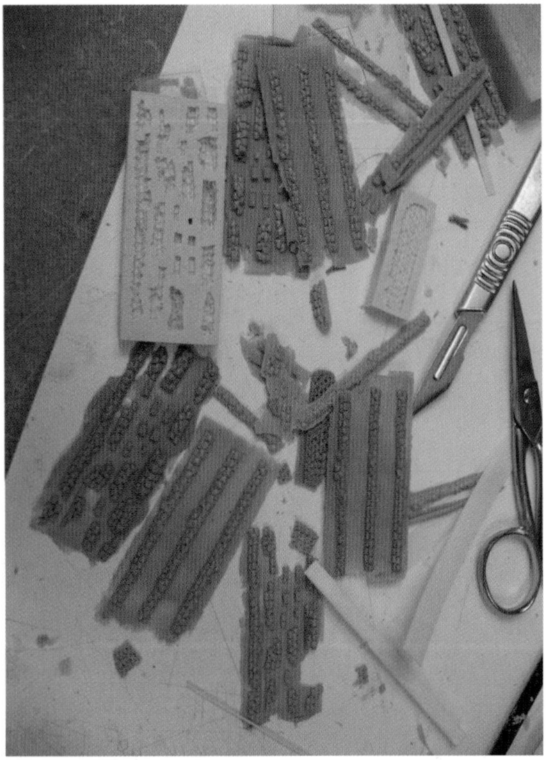

Resin castings of sandbags.

Adding filter washes of dark ochre on wooden parts and dark brown on soil areas.

so that it gave a rough, irregular finish. (This technique was refined for the 1:32 sections and you will find a fuller explanation in Chapter 2.)

Useful Tip

Styrene is best scribed using the back edge of a scalpel blade as it drags out some of the material.

Painting

Rather than painting everything with solid colour, acrylic paint filter washes can be used to bring out the detail. The model has several colours for variety: Ochre, Fawn and Raw Umber. When thinned as a 'wash' it will stain the white styrene to a yellow or greyish-brown wood colour, and where the Raw Umber wash concentrates in the grooves it gives dark brown shadows. The corrugated iron was painted with greys and dark red-browns to create a rusty look, and the revetment was dry-brushed with light grey to create highlights.

Useful Tips

A thinned paint 'filter wash' is darker where it concentrates in grooves, creating shadows, but it also tints the main surface.

Dry-brushing is a technique in which most of the paint is wiped off your brush onto a waste cloth. As the paint begins to dry on the brush, gently rub it across raised surfaces to accentuate their detail and contrast more with darker recesses. It wrecks brushes, so only use old ones.

Soil, Chalk and Grass

The groundwork was painted with a thick wash of Raw Umber to create a base colour for the soil. The groundwork was then painted with water-thinned PVA glue before finely sieved soil was sprinkled on. When laying textures, it is best done in smaller areas to avoid the glue forming a dry skin. Ideally leave a thin strip without texture where the glue was applied last, so it is still wet when you move on to the next section. This helps to avoid hard seam lines between the smaller patches that you are working in. When the 'soil' was dry, this process was repeated on the parapets and shell holes with fine chalk powder. (An explanation of how to make fine chalk will be found in Chapter 2.)

When the soil and chalk were dry, thinned PVA was painted over the main areas to glue down various 'grass' textures: it is surprising the difference green grass made to the drab model. Nylon flock has a sheen, so it was dry-brushed with Ochre and Olive Green, which also helped to vary the colour of the fields. Lastly, shell-torn trees were added, using real plant root and larger pieces of foam texture for bushes. The best principle to use is to work from the ground upwards. Start by painting the groundwork, which can be seen between the texture, and then add soil, grass, bushes and lastly trees.

Sieved soil and chalk have been fixed with diluted PVA.

Green flock grass brightens the drab palette.

Useful Tip

Nylon flock shines, so dry-brush it with matt paint after it is firmly glued in place.

Barbed Wire

Barbed wire was made from fine wire wool. It was spray-painted grey and speckled with red brown and rust orange. Hundreds of fine holes were drilled into the groundwork and wire fence posts inserted, before laying the lines of wire on top. No attempt was made to create barbs because they would be so tiny. The model has many pieces of debris like boxes, spare duckboards and smashed revetment. Trenches were usually untidy places that constantly needed repairing. Many hours were spent looking at old photos in an attempt to recreate the detail as realistically as possible in this tiny scale. Fine work is best done with watchmaker's tweezers, because fingers are just too fat.

Dugouts and positions

The walls and floors of the three dugouts on the edges of the model were detailed and painted separately before posting them in place, just for ease. Styrene furniture and figures were last to be added. The model is littered with other features like machine guns, mortars, observation posts, latrines and funk holes. Items such as Lewis guns or trench mortars are not available commercially, so had to be created mostly from styrene and wire. Other features like 'knife rests' are shown, made from styrene and fine electrical wire. These wooden frames wrapped with barbed wire would

Overview of the model from the front line.

sit above the trench and could be pulled into it quickly, blocking the area that had to be evacuated and giving the defenders vital minutes to escape safely.

Figures

There are about 100 figures on the model but, being only about 7mm tall, some people have not even noticed them. They are actually World War II British artillery figures, made by a company called GHQ for war-gaming. Because they are so small, you cannot see that they are wearing the short, buckled gaiters of that war rather than the bandage-style puttees of the Great War.

GHQ British artillery figures.

Chapter Two

Creating Groundwork on Section Models

After making my small-scale diorama, I decided to build a section model showing and describing the parts of a trench in greater detail than would be possible at 1:285 scale. As I studied what to construct, I found that there was a big difference between what the field manuals said a trench should look like and what was actually possible in battlefield conditions, so I began by making two sections: a textbook-style 'ideal' British trench and a typical example of what was usually built – too shallow, with weak revetment, and built from whatever materials the troops could get their hands on locally. A third section was soon started to show how wet soil meant that you had to build a wall above ground level rather than digging into it. I then built sections showing how French and German trenches differed. I now have ten section models, each showing different aspects of trench warfare, but the collection is not comprehensive. I could add to it, but vowed not to start any more until the present ten were finished. There are many aspects of the conflict that my models do not explain, but all the sections are based on the Western Front in France and Belgium.

WHAT TOOLS ARE NEEDED?

As a professional modelmaker, I work in a 'paradise' of facilities with model parts made on 3D printers, laser-cutters and CNC machines. Models require teamwork, but I specialize in landscaping and sculptural objects, and some of the models I have contributed to may be seen at www.3dd.co.uk. My bosses kindly allow me to use their machines in my own time. Some hobby modellers are beginning to get access to this new way and we are now getting 3D sculpted and printed models. It is the future.

My final three section models had to be completed during the 2020 Covid-19 'lockdown' and I was forced to set up a makeshift workbench on the end of my dining table, where there is plenty of light and air. This gave me a renewed glimpse of how the average hobby modelmaker works at home and the main key is improvisation. The first thing I did was to put a sheet of polythene over the table because spills of paint or glue are unpredictable. You will notice from many of my progress photos through the book that I always work on cutting boards, which come in a variety of sizes. At home, I have an A2-sized one double-sided to a wooden board, giving me a self-healing working surface to cut on and not be too concerned about.

The most essential tools as far as I am concerned are scalpel, steel rule, engineer's square and tweezers. I have been accumulating hand tools for more than forty years and so have hundreds of tools for numerous tasks. As I have got older, with my eyesight faltering, I need the aid of an Optivisor to see small intricate work well. Good tweezers enable me to handle tiny objects, too small to handle with fingers. As your desire to adapt models grows you will want more handy tools

Versatile workspace – an A2-sized cutting board fixed to an MDF board (with the board removed it became an artist's easel). The section models had to be completed with what I could find at home. Core tools used were tweezers, steel rule, scalpel and engineer's square.

like needle files, pliers, fine scissors, a razor saw, a palette knife, a pin vice and small drills. Sculpting tools become necessary when you venture into the world of modelling putties, but you can improvise with a needle stuck into a plastic or wooden handle. Files of all sorts of sizes can be made by double-siding sandpaper to bits of wood or plastic and you can even use nail files. (Note that cutting sandpaper wrecks scalpel blades.)

Hobby power tools like Dremels come with a host of helpful burrs and cutting blades, but you must be careful. I have a 70mm scar on my right thumb from a moment's lack of attention and an almost career-changing accident, which happened so quickly! I have two further scars from the same momentary lapse that resulted in 21 stitches needed within five seconds, so think before you act.

Of course paints and brushes are essential tools too. I use acrylic paint mostly, but oil paint is used for specific tasks. Good brushes with a fine point are invaluable and you will need to treat your brushes with care to keep their useful tips. (An explanation of the basics of figure painting will be found in Chapter 11.)

A collection of useful tools: (top) Dremel with burrs; (middle) home-made sanding boards/sticks, needle files, Optivisor; (bottom) pliers, razor saw, palette knife, steel rule, tweezers, scalpel, sculpting tool, scissors, pin vice and drills, Optivisor lenses.

BASIC SHAPES OF THE SECTION MODELS

As an architectural modelmaker I can use small off-cuts of scrap material for my own projects and I have access to all the machinery I could ever wish for. I build the bulk of my bases from sheet acrylic (perspex), but it would be possible to replicate what I do in other materials like styrene or plywood. I've been able to create display boxes using black MDF and selecting prints of World War I battle scenes to act as backdrops. Each model is lit with 12-volt LED strip from above and the interior models have 'warm' LED lighting inside.

Useful Tip

One of the keys to being a good modelmaker is being adaptable. There are usually several ways to get a task done. Find and use methods with which you are happy and confident.

The basic rectangles of the bases are cut from 3mm acrylic sheet using a circular saw. Curved shapes are then cut with a bandsaw. If you do not have access to machines like this, then hand tools like a coping saw will do the job. The back and front sides of the sections were cut first, along with strips of 44mm-wide acrylic for making the sides, bottom and tops. (The 44mm strip, along with 3mm front and back, make each section 50mm deep.)

The basic shapes of the sections are constructed in 3mm acrylic sheet.

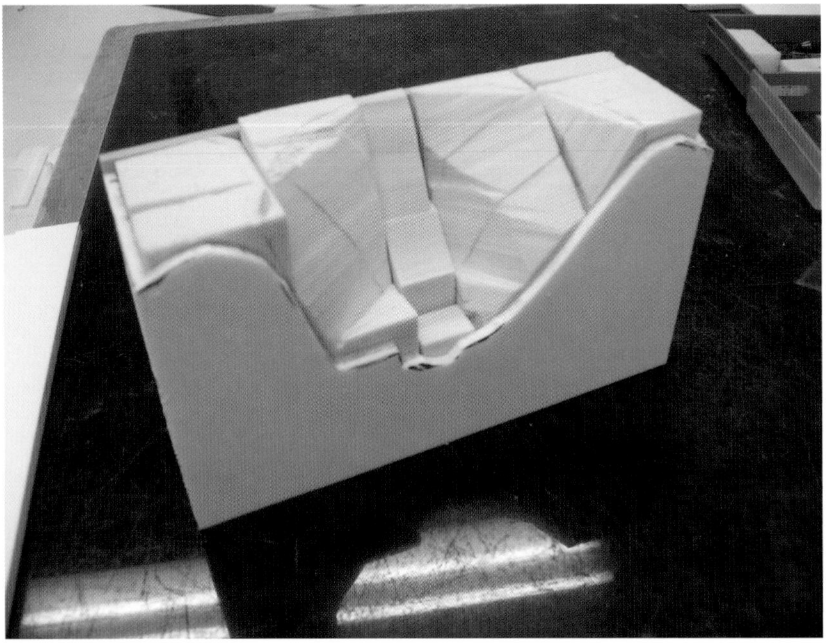

The shell hole base was carved from pieces of polyurethane inside the acrylic shell.

Most of the sections are 150mm wide, but the British wet soil trench and German bunker were extended to 200mm. After cutting the base piece and two ends, the profile of the groundwork and trench was formed with short pieces of the 44mm strip. They were cut and glued in line with flat areas, but put slightly below a contoured surface that does not need to be perfect, as this is covered with soil or revetment.

Making the Shell Hole Base

The basic box shape of the shell hole model was made with the usual 3mm sheet acrylic, but it was filled with low density polyurethane foam due to the complexity of its shape. (This is a product purchased in large, expensive sheets, so well beyond what a hobbyist would be able to justify.) Insulation foam is a similar type of plastic and this was used because the concave surface could be easily carved and sanded to shape, before coating it with car body filler. (A word of warning: the resin in car body filler will melt expanded polystyrene.) The German bunker was built with blocks of high density polyurethane, as it was the easiest way to make it.

MY 'SOIL' TECHNIQUE

After making the basic shapes of the trench from sheet acrylic, the soil contours were formed with a thin layer of car body filler. This is a polyurethane resin-based product that really stinks and is poisonous, so make sure that you work in a well-ventilated area. After a first thin layer, a second thin coat is added using a technique that I discovered by chance. Car body filler goes crumbly and crystalline as the catalyst takes effect and it begins to harden. There is only a very short 'window' of time to work in, so you have to be quick, working in small areas with small amounts of curing filler. If you look at the unpainted models, you will notice the varying shades of grey to pink, depending on how much catalyst has been added. (The catalyst is red, so the more catalyst added, the pinker it becomes and the quicker it will harden.) It needs a bit of experimentation to master this technique, but it creates realistic-looking grains for loose soil. Dry Polyfilla can also be added as another variation, because broken soil has many sizes of texture.

Contoured surfaces are formed from short lengths of acrylic, covered with a thin coat of car body filler.

A layer of 'curing' filler is applied in small areas. Note the varying shades of pink, depending on how much red catalyst was added.

Painting Soil

When the bases are ready, a base coat of grey primer and then light (Moonstone) grey was sprayed using cellulose paint. All pieces of timber or twigs for logs were kept loose until the groundwork had been spray painted. So that they are not fixed in place with car body filler, they can be wrapped with adhesive tape before surrounding them, as this will stop it bonding to them. Once they are base coated the loose parts were glued with PVA and the gaps filled with Polyfilla. Detail was accentuated in emulsion and acrylic paint.

Wooden pieces are kept loose until the base coat has been sprayed. The gaps are then filled with dry Polyfilla.

Several washes of Raw Umber (dark brown) were applied, which sinks into all the recesses. Some areas got more wash than others to vary the background colour of the groundwork, which was then dry-brushed and detailed with several shades of light brown and grey. Further washes and highlights were applied until the desired effect was achieved. Do not blanket colour the whole model, but rather have areas of darker, damp soil among lighter-coloured areas of dry soil.

Useful Tips

Generally avoid white paint except for extreme highlights, and use very dark brown instead of black for shadows as this looks more natural.

Other modelmakers prefer to add sand or cat litter to paint to make a textured paste that can be applied to areas of soil. Textured paint dries up in its pot quite quickly and does not store well.

All soil areas are given a thinned wash of Raw Umber paint.

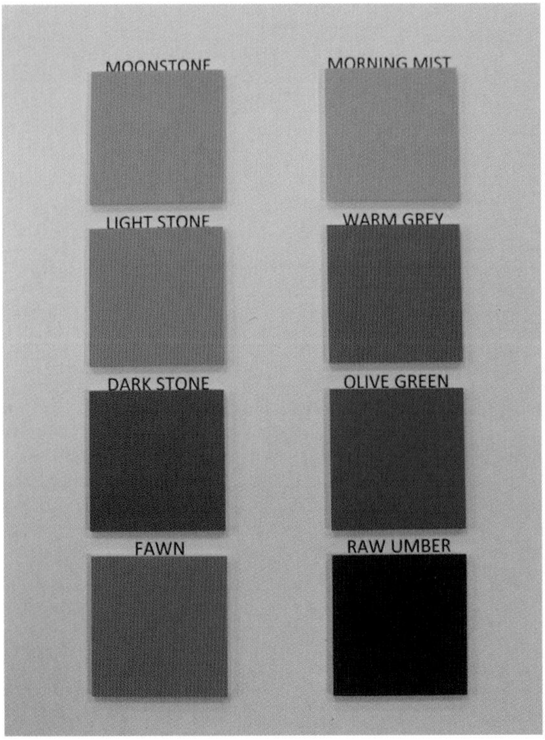

Basic palette of colours used on the groundwork.

Look for the variance in the soil texture and colour. Dark, wet soil spills from broken sandbags. Root and etched weeds have been added.

Soil has differing texture and colour depending on how damp it is, as seen at Andy Robertshaw's 24 Hour Trench in his garden in Surrey.

Textured paint can be made by adding fine sand, but paints with added texture will dry up in the bottles much more quickly than standard acrylic paint, so be aware that your paint may not last for many months. You can buy ready-made textured paint, but this too has a short shelf life. Reality in Scale (www.realityinscale.com) and AMMO (www.migjimenez.com) make textured paints that are good for painting on tools or equipment splattered with mud. If you study a garden tool with mud on it you will find that mud will dry at the edges first before the central core dries up. This means that there will be lighter dry mud around the edges and darker wetter mud in the centre.

Wet Soil and Water

If you study puddles as you go for walks you will notice that the wet soil surrounding the puddle is darker. The water becomes a translucent light brown colour or green if it becomes stagnant.

There are many products available on the modelmaking market for making water, but you can also experiment with products created for artists, such as acrylic gloss medium or acrylic

Note the mixture of gloss and matt surfaces on the wet floor of the 24 Hour Trench.

Some areas are damp, dark and shiny, whereas higher surfaces have been dry-brushed to appear dry, lighter and matt.

gloss gel, which are made to add bulk and translucency to artist's paint. Many of these products are white, but dry clear or translucent. Adding paint to these products will create translucent colours ideal for puddles, but they look better if you apply a few clear coats on top to give some depth.

After painting 'wet' areas of mud with gloss lacquer, dry-brush some of the upstanding soil with slightly lighter brown acrylic paint to create dryer matt soil among the glossy wet patches. The higher soil will dry more quickly while the soil next to the puddles remains wet and darker.

Useful Tips

Dry-brush glossed 'wet' soil with matt paint to make it look as if some is drying out. The contrast between gloss and matt adds realism.

When you are out walking or in a garden, look for natural products like grasses or small leaves that look like scaled-down versions. Why waste time trying to make something if the real thing can be adapted?

Deep water can be created by forming the main bulk from thin sheets of acrylic that have their undersurface painted brown. Onto this apply several coats of acrylic gloss medium to give even more depth and an uneven surface. You will find that acrylic resin or acrylic gel shrinks as it dries, so it has to be applied in several thin coats. Trying to apply a single thick coat will just cause the resin to crack and distort as it shrinks.

Using Real Soil and Stones

Some of these models use real sieved soil or small stones. Dust swept from a garden path is mostly soil, but can contain grains of several colours. It is best sieved to remove unwanted larger lumps. Some modelmakers are concerned about using natural products because they can contain living organisms, but this can be solved by placing the dust into a microwave and briefly 'nuking' anything that it might contain. The French section (*see* Chapter 9) contains small lumps of buff-coloured sandstone among the car body filler to make a more stony soil. Model groundwork can look very bland or uniform, but adding variation within their surfaces will give a more natural realism.

Real chalk, 'flint' and soil have been added to this trench section.

Chalky soil usually contains flint, which can be easily created using real stones. Broken shingle or gravel stones look like small pieces of flint when it is broken up with a hammer. Before you start hitting small stones with a hammer you should be warned of some safety issues. It will break into small sharp pieces that fly in all directions, so you should wear some eye protection, just in case. Cut the base off a paper cup, just shorter than the length of your hammer's head, to create a skirt around the stones you are trying to smash. This way, the pieces may fly in all directions but the skirt will contain them and will save you time trying to find the pieces, as well as being safer. You will also need to find a hard surface like concrete to work on or you will end up creating dents in something softer like a wooden floor. A last useful tip is to smash them on top of a sheet of scrap paper. It will get damaged, but will stay intact enough to allow you to tip the contents into a sealable bag or container.

Small gravel stones are suitable as flints.

Smashing 'flints' safely inside a skirt made from a cut-down paper cup.

Using Real Chalk

Chalky soil has been recreated on a number of the models, often using real sieved chalk to add to the paintwork. Small pieces of chalk were crushed in an old, hand-cranked mincing machine, which grinds the chalk into powder and small pieces. After grinding the chalk, sieve it with a large gauged sieve and then another with a finer mesh, like an old tea strainer. The result will be chalk, ranging from fine powder to small lumps of chalk about 1–1.5mm. Chalk can also be cut with a scalpel into lumps about 3 or 4mm in size. These can be stored in sealable bags ready for use.

Old meat mincer, used to grind chalk into powder.

Sieving chalk with two gauges of sieve.

Chalk Parados Base

Chalk is a soft rock and you will find photos of some trenches with little or no revetment. This figure base was sprayed with a basecoat of Moonstone grey cellulose paint before working with acrylic paints, applied with brushes. It is best to avoid harsh black shadows and opt for a wash of very dark brown, which settles into the recesses, bringing out some of the detail. The 'chalk' was created with a mixture of dry-brushing or stippling with white and warm white. A chalk wall is rarely a uniform colour, so further washes or 'filters' of brown and yellow-brown were applied to create the varying tones. Pure white was saved for the extreme highlights.

Excavated chalk at Hawthorne Trench, Kent.

Chalk parados base with added chalk, texture, root and weeds.

Chalk parados base, showing the paintwork before textures were added.

When happy with the paintwork, real chalk and sieved soil can be added, fixing the dust or fine texture with acrylic matt medium. When applying powder it is easiest to sprinkle the dust in place and then paint acrylic matt medium over it. Larger pieces of chalk or flint are best glued with PVA.

Useful Tips

Always work with bits of paper underneath your model, so that the remains of the textures can be tipped back into sealable bags when you have finished, ready for the next time they are needed.

Find a way to organize your scenic textures so that you can find them easily when you want them.

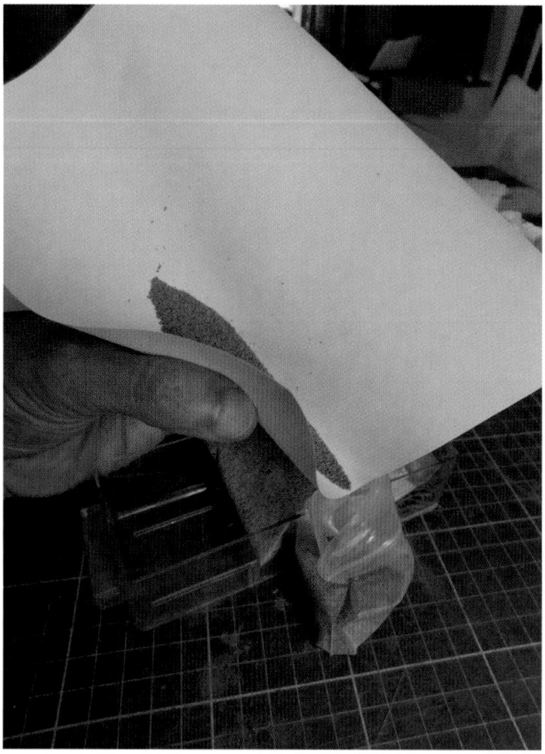

Saving the excess for later use.

A unit of small drawers like this is a good investment.

PLANTS AND GRASS

Groundwork will look even better if you add pieces of etched and laser-cut plant or fine green texture. The browns and greys of Great War models can be very dull, so adding a little interest with coloured weeds and grass is refreshing. You will find many small bits of vegetation growing on these models and many are made using natural dried grasses and leaves that have been found as I work in my garden or out for walks in the country. If an area has been excavated, then roots will emerge from the sides of the hole. Save fine plant roots while you work in your garden, but allow them to dry out before selecting the best bits for your models. There are several shell-torn tree stumps on the models, made from twigs with a fine texture that could be emphasized with dry-brushing. Grass can be made from many types of fibre such as sisal, which you can purchase from craft shops. (For information about laser-cut plants, and making dandelions or laying grass, *see* Chapters 12 and 13, respectively.)

USEFUL TIPS

Flat leaves look very unnatural, so make sure that etched or laser-cut leaves are bent at differing angles and the stems twisted round. Bending spines along the centre of a leaf will also help.

Weeds grow quickly, so do not be scared to add coloured plants, which will create interest and lift the bland palette of World War I scenes.

Chapter Three

'Ideal' British Trench

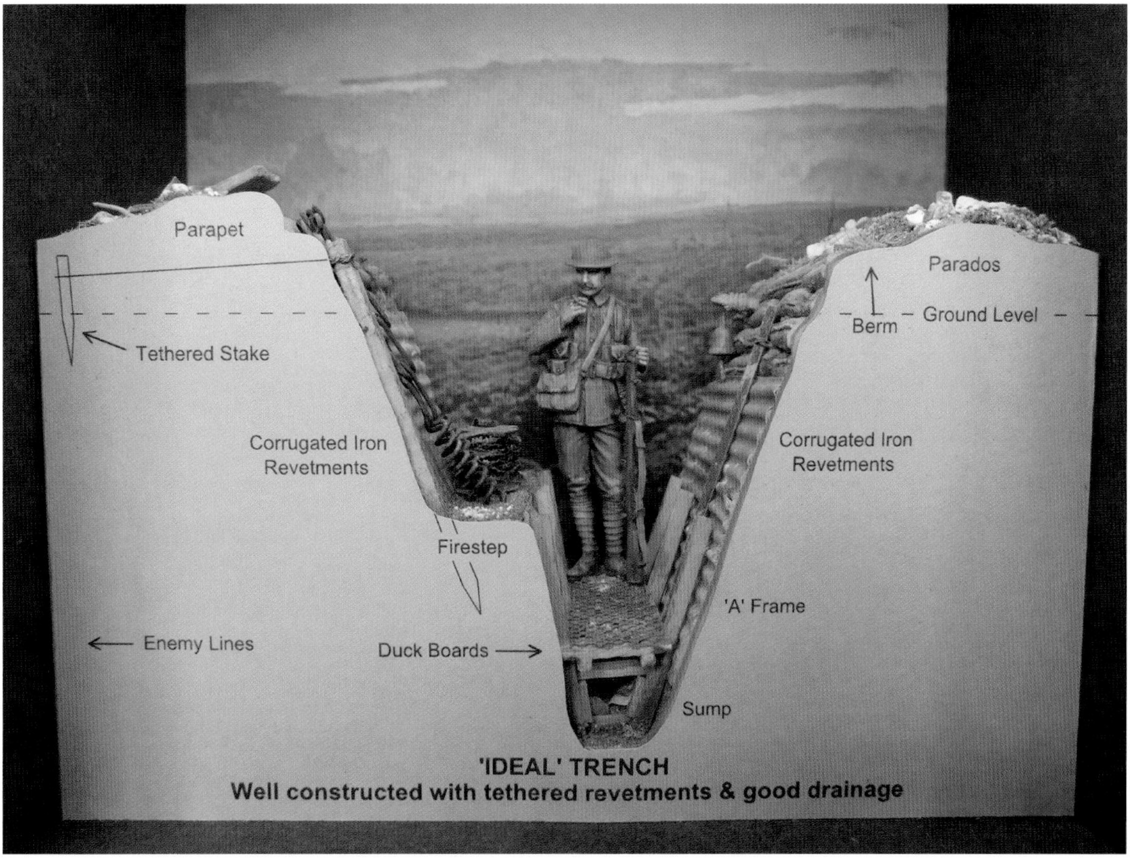

'Ideal' British Trench in its display box.

This section model represents a well-built, text-book-style British trench of the Great War, built as the field manuals said it should be. The British were able to use much more corrugated iron (nicknamed 'crinkly tin') than the Germans, who were starved of resources by the British naval blockade. Therefore, it was typically more British than German. The sheets were held in place by vertical wooden posts or angle iron, which were hammered into the ground and tethered at the top to keep the trench walls firm. Tethers were made from strong wire, attached to wooden pegs that were hammered into the ground and covered with the soil from the trench excavation. The tops of the trench walls are supported with sandbags and the parapet has an 'elbow rest', with the top layer of sandbags being set forward creating a more comfortable space from which to fire a rifle. The parados heap is piled a little higher than the parapet, making it a little harder to distinguish the silhouette of a head peeping over the parapet. Even so, a wise soldier would not put his head above the parapet during daylight as snipers were usually on the lookout. A small area at ground level, called a berm, is left between the rear vertical wall and the parados soil heap, making it less likely for soil to gravitate back into the trench.

This trench floor is lined with wooden A-frames, which support the trench walls but also create a sump where rainwater can drain. (They were named A-frames because they are shaped like an upside-down A.) The upper cross-brace forms a frame to support a higher walkway of duckboards over the sump. Wet wood can be very slippery, so the boards are covered with chicken wire for grip. The trench is deep enough (at least 6ft or 1.83m) so that a soldier standing on the duckboards has his head sheltered safely within the trench walls.

On the firestep is a small reel of barbed wire and steel screw pickets, waiting to be used to reinforce the band of barbed wire, sited several yards in front of the trench to prevent an attacking enemy from getting close to the trench. Originally wooden posts were hammered into the ground to suspend the wire from. Wiring had to be done at night, but it was dangerous as each side would listen for

Offset joist duckboards on A-frames, at Hawthorne Trench, Kent.

British trench with A-frames and tapered joist duckboards, Memorial Museum Passchendaele 1917.

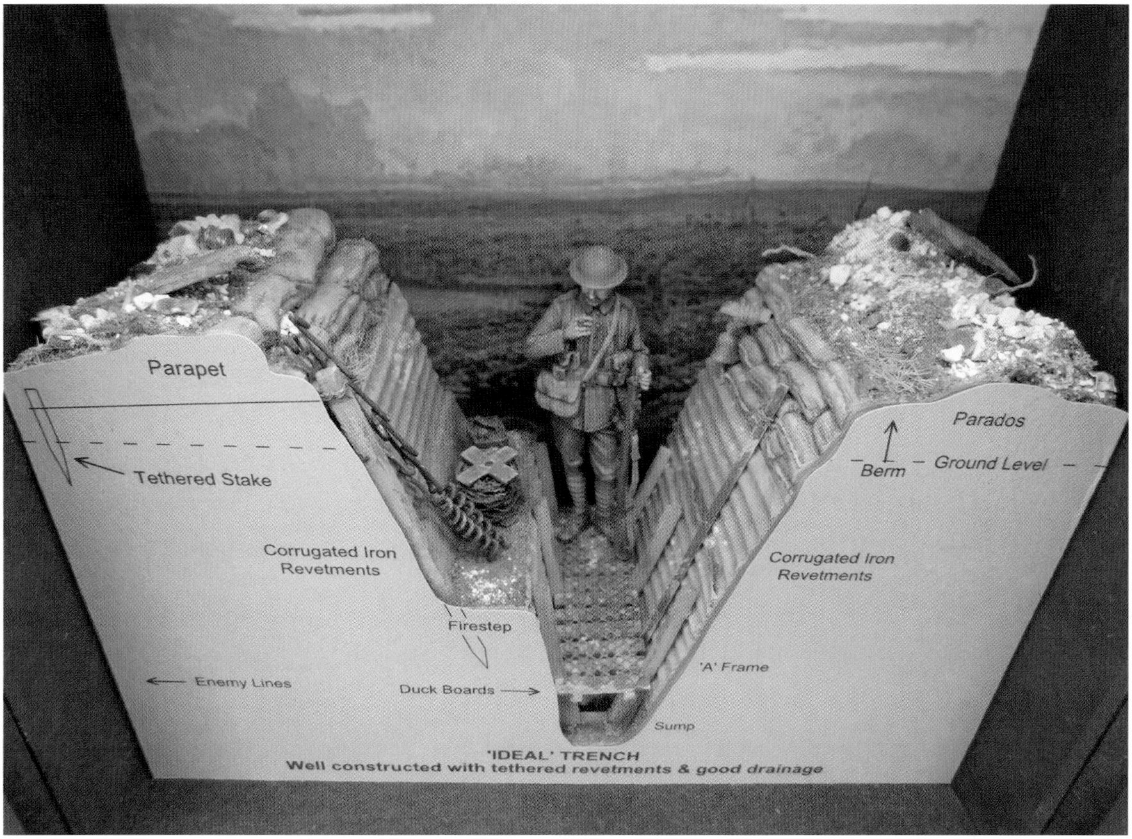

The parados soil pile is slightly higher than the parapet to help disguise a head that appeared above it.

noise and attack an enemy who was making his position stronger. Flares were sent up regularly to light up the area and hamper any progress. Troops would be forced to stand like statues, in the hope of not being spotted. Banging wooden posts into the soil with a mallet would be noisy, even when muffled with sackcloth, so the metal screw picket was designed with several rings on its upper shaft, through which barbed wire could be fixed. The rings were also used to insert a lever so that it could be corkscrewed into the ground quietly. Next to the screw pickets is a 'flimsy' petrol can; these were reused to bring water up to the front lines (*see* Chapter 5).

The soldier wears standard British equipment, including a PH hood satchel, which was the first type of gas mask used when chlorine gas was introduced in 1915. He risks smoking, which was unwise in the front line as rising smoke shows the enemy where the trench is occupied and could attract rifle grenades or mortars.

CORRUGATED IRON

Corrugated iron was supplied in sheets 2ft 9in wide and in 6ft, 7ft or 9ft lengths. Scale corrugated iron sheets can be created with metal foil using formers made of 2mm styrene rods, interspersed with 1mm square sections, fixed to stronger 3mm pieces of acrylic. When a piece of aluminium foil is placed between the two formers and squeezed with pliers in each corner, the foil becomes corrugated. The formers shown are large enough to make a scale 2ft 9in × 6ft sheet (26.2 × 57.24mm at 1:32 scale). Aluminium foil keeps its shape, but you can also pierce it for shell damage or rust holes. Ready-made corrugated sheet is available from Historex Agents, made by Reality in Scale, if creating your own seems too much trouble.

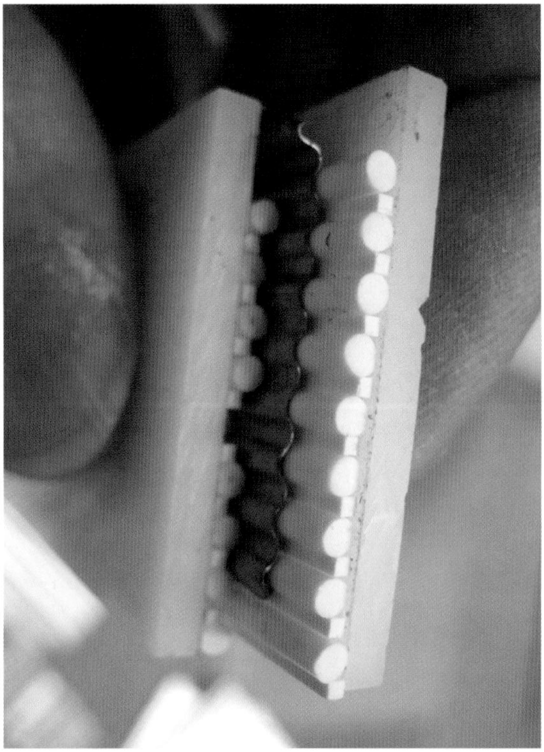

Styrene formers for creating corrugated aluminium foil.

Cutting pie-tin foil for corrugated iron sheets.

Corrugated foil after being pressed within the formers.

The model before painting.

DUCKBOARDS

Mud is very sticky and hampers movement. Duckboards, ideally covered with chicken wire for grip, were made to cover the trench floor, giving a firm path to walk on. Rows of parallel boards were nailed to larger joists below, with gaps between to allow rainwater to drain off. In areas where rainwater gathered, the boards were raised off the wet ground on A-frames. Duckboards were made close to the front lines by engineers and carried forward by the troops. They were usually about 2ft wide and their length could vary between 6ft and 8ft. British engineers came up with clever ways to secure the lengths of board together. One method was to taper the joists, so that one end was wider than the other. At the thin end, the joists would continue without boards on top, so that it could be inserted between the joists of the wider end of the next duckboard. Another method was to have joists offset, so that the boards overhang on one side about the width of a joist. If the boards were laid with the offset on alternate sides, the joists would interlink and create a stronger connection between boards. Both types of board and their joining techniques are shown on the bases. A 1:32 scale duckboard will be about 15mm × 57–76mm long.

Duckboards I have created for Tommy's War masters, which are intended to be cast, are created from 1mm acrylic with laser-etched wood grain on their surface. A number of small boards are cut about 3 × 15mm, and glued to joists of about 2.5 × 3mm. Creating a jig helps to make many boards of the same length, with boards spaced at

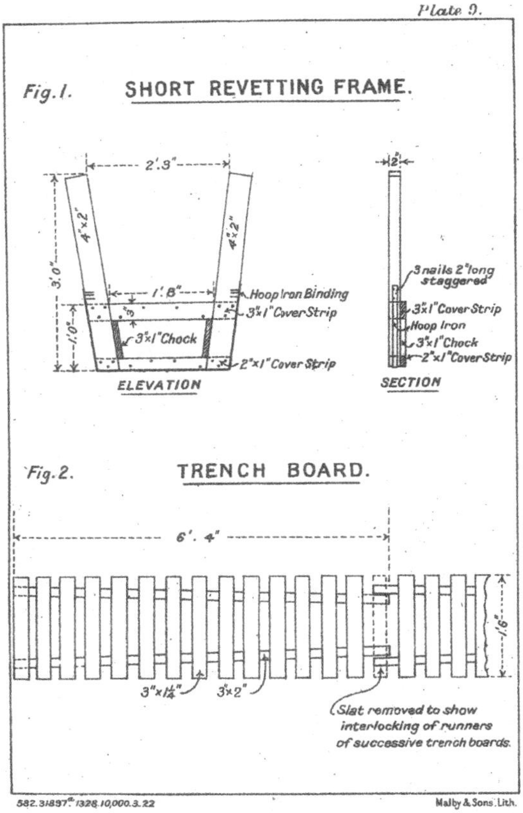

Plan of A-frames and tapered duckboards, from the War Office's Manual of Fieldworks (All Arms), *1921.*

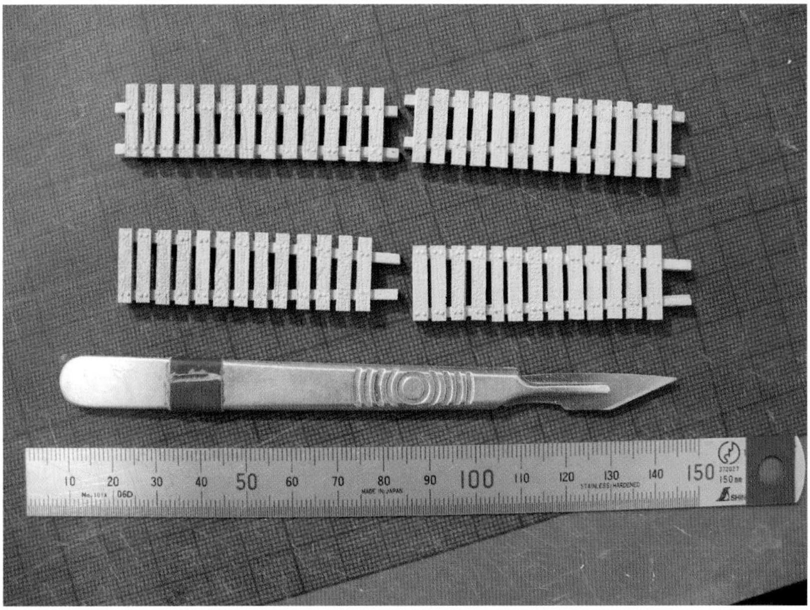

Offset and tapered duckboards: masters made for Tommy's War.

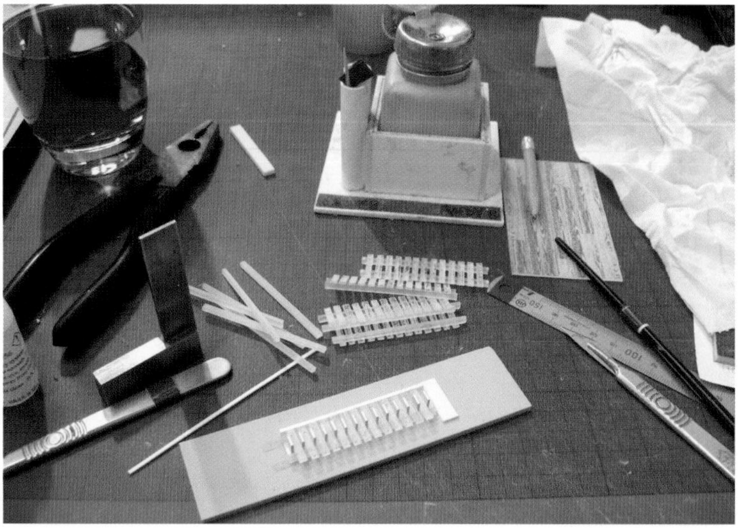

Jig for making acrylic offset duckboards.

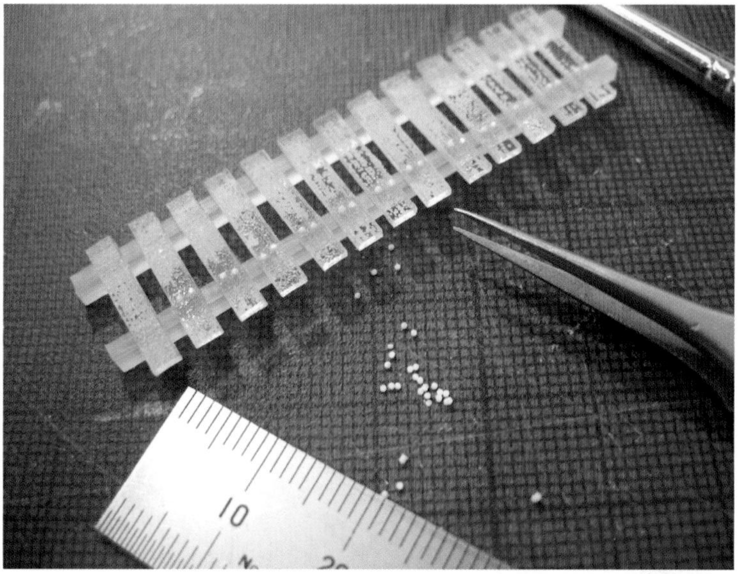

Adding 'nails' made from small slivers of 0.5mm styrene rod.

regular intervals. The most boring part of acrylic duckboard production is adding nail heads. Each of the small boards needs four nails, so a 6ft length will have over fifty nails. Tiny discs for nail heads can be made from 0.5mm styrene rod. Cutting 0.5mm lengths with a scalpel, they have to be picked up, one at a time, and glued in place. You will discover that it is best to put them in place dry and then paint solvent on top to avoid them being glued to the tweezers or put solvent onto the board and then put the nail into the pool of glue.

Useful Tip

Paint balsa with a thinned wash of paint, which highlights its natural grain.

For my personal models I prefer to make duckboards using balsa wood. Balsa has the advantage that, if you snap it carefully, it will give you a true ragged edge because it has wood grain. You will find that applying thin washes of paint on balsa, rather than 'blanket' painting it, will accentuate its natural grain. When you apply a wash of paint to balsa, fibres rise and it will look hairy. Wait until the paint has dried and gently rub the surface with your finger or fine sandpaper so the raised fibres either fall off or lay back down. The vibrancy of the colour will dull overnight too, so it may need a second coat of wash. The colour of wood can vary a lot between beige when newly sawn, to grey brown when old and weathered. Adding ochre, brown or grey washes of acrylic paint to different parts of the same wood will look more natural. For 'nails', drill 0.5mm holes into the wood and insert short lengths of 0.5mm styrene rod, which stand slightly higher than the board's surface. If possible, use red-brown styrene rod as this is an appropriate base colour for old rust.

You will notice that the proportions of the A-frames on this model differ from the *Manual of Fieldworks* drawing. This section was created well before discovering the drawings with dimensions, so the A-frames or duckboard sizes were all guessed. The woodwork was all made locally and you will notice that the A-frames shown at Yorkshire Trench, Ypres, have different proportions to those in the engineer's drawing.

Duckboards on A-frames to keep the boards dry, Yorkshire Trench, Ypres, Belgium.

STEEL SCREW PICKETS

The metal screw picket was introduced in 1916 and had several rings on its upper shaft, through which barbed wire could be fixed. Screw pickets were made of half-inch mild steel and came in three lengths: 5ft 7in (with three or four loops), 3ft 9in and 2ft 1in (both with one or two loops).

At 1:32 scale a 5ft 7in long picket with three or four loops will be 53mm. A medium picket will be 36mm long and a short picket will be 20mm long. 1mm copper wire was used to make the pickets shown, but 30amp fuse wire will do just as well. The ground screw was created by twisting the wire around a 1.5mm rod, which was also used to make each of the loops. If your pickets are to be fixed in the ground, then there is no need to make the screw part, which is hidden in the ground.

Screw picket and barbed wire at Hawthorne Trench, Kent.

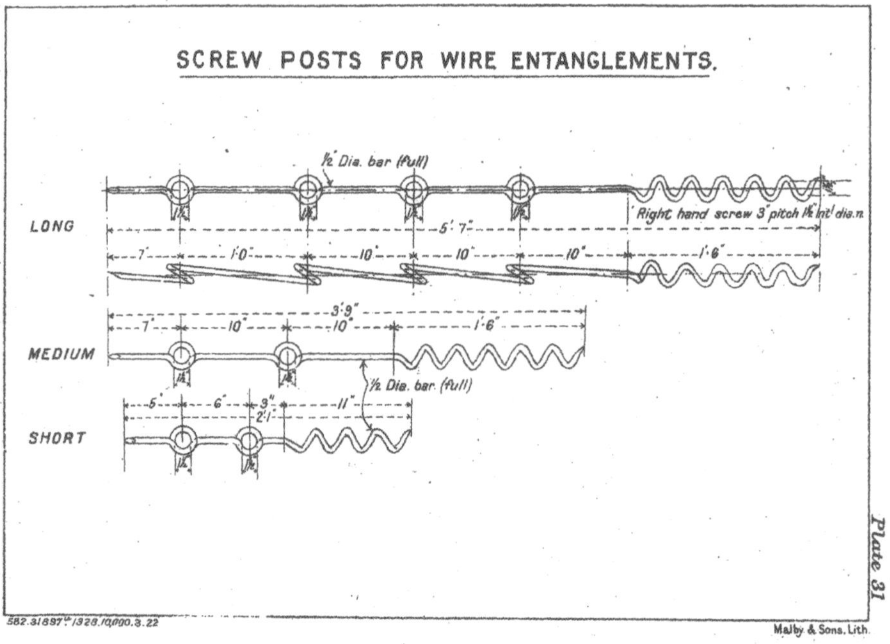

Plan of screw pickets, from the Manual of Fieldworks (All Arms)*, 1921.*

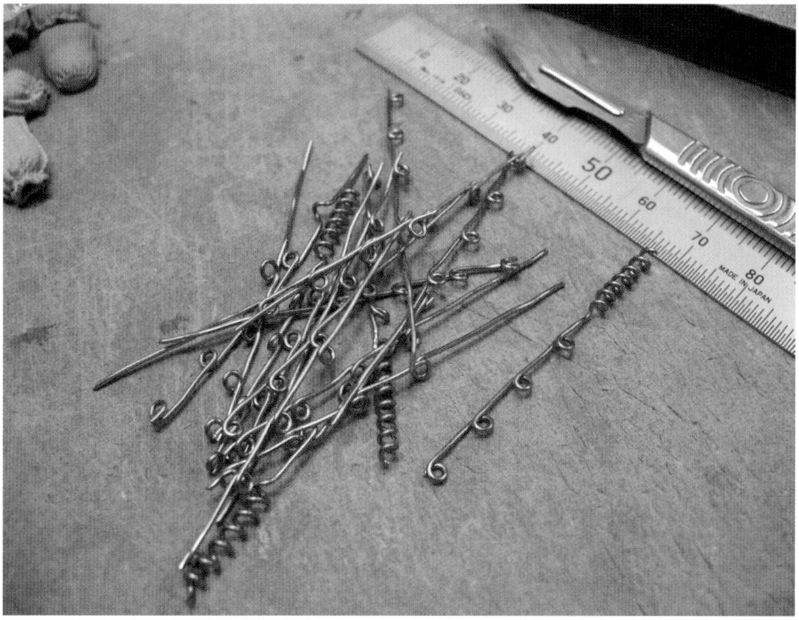

Screw pickets made from copper wire.

CREATING A BARBED WIRE REEL

On the firestep, next to the screw pickets, is a small reel of barbed wire. Barbed wire was carried into the front lines in many different ways. Photos show large reels carried by pairs of soldiers, suspended between them on a pole, or carried over the shoulder; smaller quantities were also transported. Some reels were just a few bits of wood nailed roughly together but others, like the one created here, were a bit more refined. This reel has half-lap jointed wooden sides to keep the wire in place and a hole through its core to aid the dispensing of the wire. The reel sides were made from 0.5mm styrene, butt jointed and glued with solvent. The sides are 12mm long, so each side was made up of a 12mm length of 4mm wide styrene with two 4mm squares glued on to make the cross. These were glued to an 8mm length of 5mm styrene cylinder, around which the wire could be wound.

The 1:35 scale brass etched barbed wire shown is made by the Czech company Eduard, who produce an etched sheet of wire that snakes backwards and forwards. If bent straight, it could make one 8m length. The difference between 1:35 and 1:32 scales (used on my models) is usually too great, as it makes most accessories too small, but I considered it acceptable in this case.

Barbs usually come in fours, with one pair sitting at angles to the other. If you take the time to go along the length of wire with two pairs of fine tweezers, bending each set of barbs so that one pair points about 90 degrees to the other, the wire looks more realistic. Also twist the wire along its length, so that their carrying wire looks more like the two lengths of twisted wire. The best way to twist the etch along its length is to insert one end into a pin vice and twist manually. (An electric drill would be quicker, but would probably be too violent for this action.)

Generally, German barbed wire had more barbs and was of a thicker gauge than British wire. The Germans also tended to lay wider bands of wire, because they were usually defensive on the Western Front. The Hindenburg Line was notorious for its huge defences of barbed wire. Barbed wire was originally invented as cheap fencing for the cattle ranches of the USA, but military tacticians soon realized its value for battlefield defence and it had a huge impact on the battlefield until inventions like the tank were introduced.

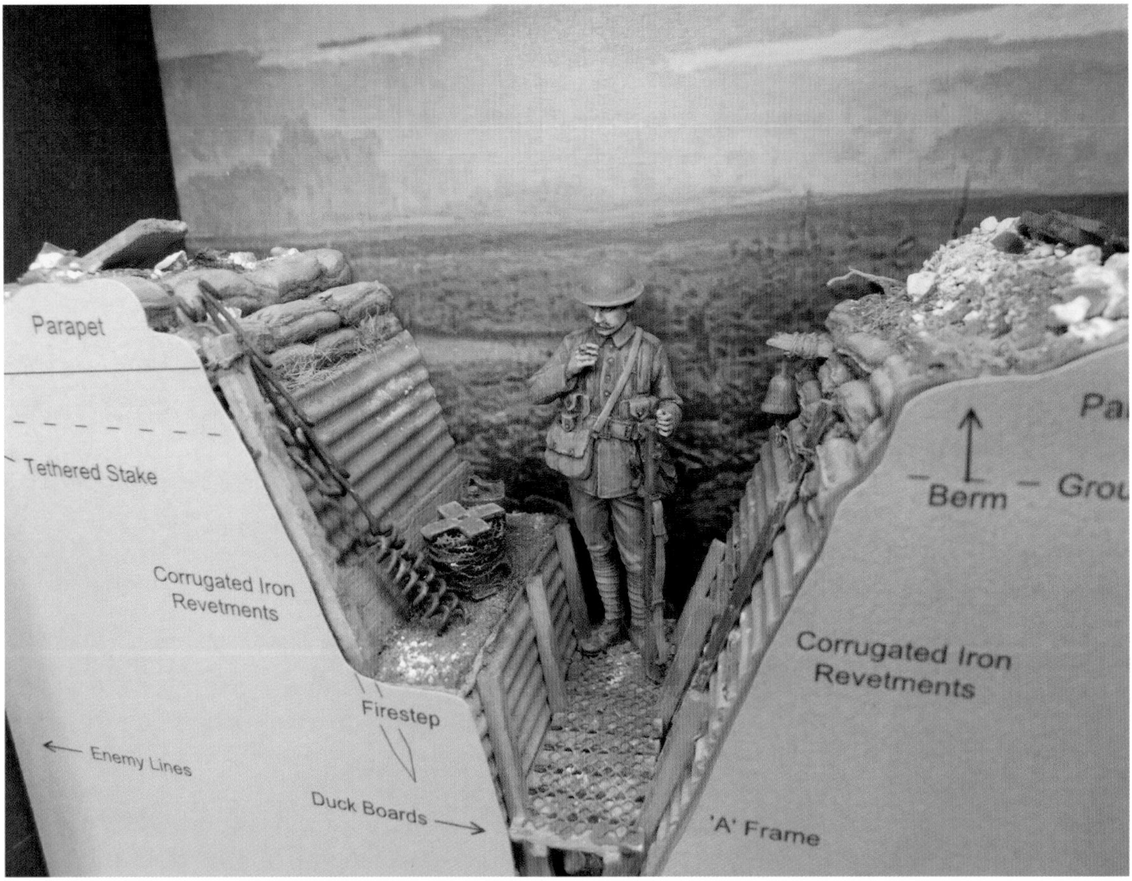

The model showing screw pickets and barbed wire reel waiting on the firestep.

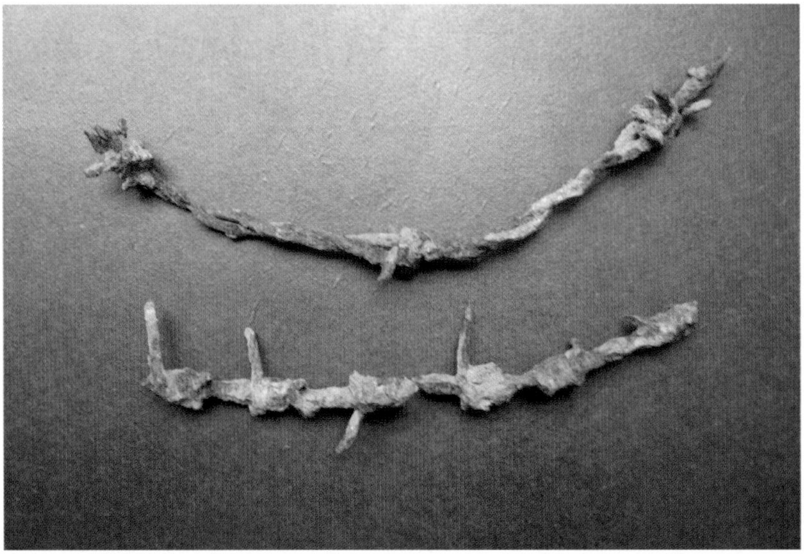

German barbed wire was usually stronger and had more barbs than British wire.

ADAPTED FIGURE

Figures give models scale and bring a human connection. Most of the figures on these models are from the Tommy's War range, but when the first sections were created the only figures available had early-war peaked caps. These figures were adapted slightly by giving them 'Brodie' helmets and mid-war gas hood satchels, but Tommy's War now produce figures with Brodies and gas hoods. This soldier was originally a Canadian soldier (TW32016), but his collar was converted to the British style and his webbing completed because it was missing behind a back pack that was omitted. The order of his personal equipment, hanging from the webbing, was also rearranged. The new collar and webbing straps were sculpted with Milliput. Buckles were added, made from bent copper wire. The figure came supplied with a Canadian Ross rifle, so it was replaced with a British Lee Enfield rifle from my spares box. The wisp of cigarette smoke is made from wool from a cotton bud.

USEFUL TIP

It is quite easy and rewarding to adapt a stock figure by changing his head or moving his arms slightly, giving them your own character and pose.

Completed webbing on the figure, sculpted with Milliput.

Chapter Four

Typical British Trench

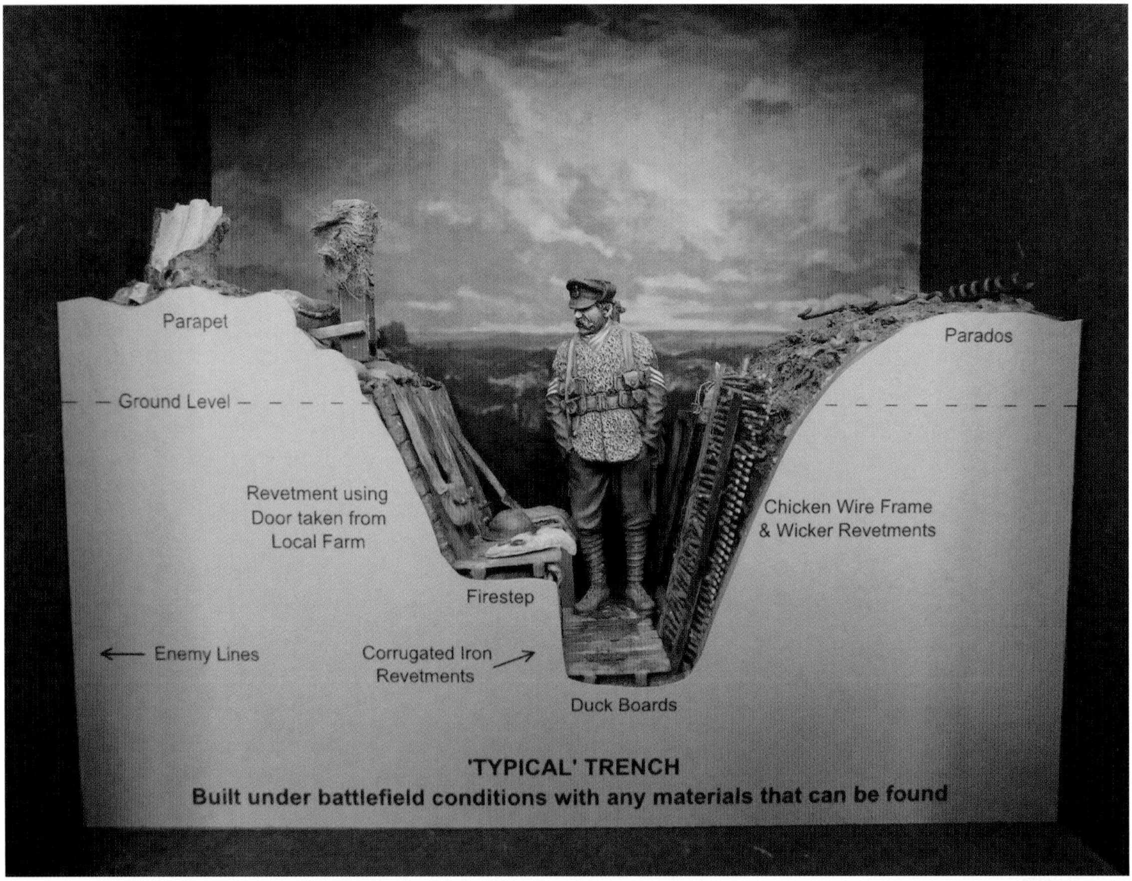

Typical British Trench in its display box.

This typical British trench is too shallow and the soldier is in danger of having his brains blown out because he is distracted and has failed to stoop. (An old sergeant would probably be wiser.) Trenches dug and repaired under the threat of shellfire were usually far from perfect and the revetment shown is made from a mixture of materials. Troops had to utilize anything they could get their hands on, so the parapet wall has been revetted with an old wooden door, taken from a nearby farm building. The rear parados wall has been revetted with a wicker hurdle and a chicken wire frame. Woven twigs or a wooden frame covered with chicken wire offer basic support to the soil walls, but will need regular repair as none is tethered or strong. Having no sump, the partially flooded trench floor would be slippery as the duckboards have no chicken-wire covering.

There are some empty sandbags on the fire-step waiting to be filled, to help raise the height of the parapet. Sandbags were made of a single piece of hessian sackcloth, folded in half, with a seam sown on one side and one end. When full, the open end could be tied or just folded over. They were transported to the front empty and filled with soil from where they were being used. Ideally they would be filled with the seam turned inside, to last longer, but photos show this rarely happened in practice because repair work was done at night and tired soldiers would simply want to get the task finished. Unless a strict officer or NCO was in charge, then bags would be filled and piled as soon as possible. The bags were placed on top of each other, overlapping like brick courses and then bedded together by bashing a spade on top in an attempt to reduce subsidence, as their contents settled over time. The wall of bags would be built slanting backwards so that gravity would pull them against the soil wall it was supporting. Some sandbags were placed end on, so that they sat within the soil behind, giving an extra key to hold them firm.

Fixed into the parapet by a spike in its base is a box periscope. It was usually too dangerous to expose your head above the parapet in daylight but it was also important to keep a constant watch on enemy lines to check for early signs of danger. Both sides would have hidden snipers, waiting for

Members of the 10th Essex Regt (Pete and Max Birkett) in Andy Robertshaw's 24 Hour Trench, Surrey.

A pile of empty sandbags await filling to raise the parapet height.

soldiers who unwisely showed themselves. Even periscopes were shot at, to blind your enemy, so these were often camouflaged with sackcloth.

The sergeant looks down despondently at his new equipment, first issued to British troops in 1915. The 'Brodie' helmet was given to the soldiers because there were so many head wounds. The shape of the British helmet continued to be used until World War II, but it offered little protection to the back of the neck. A Brodie could not stop a bullet that hit it straight on, but it did protect the head from shrapnel or flying debris. Soldiers can often be seen with the chin strap sitting behind their heads due to a fear that the blast from a nearby explosion could snap your neck.

Next to the helmet on the firestep is a PH gas hood. A soldier would breathe in through the treated cloth of the hood and exhale through his mouth via the rubber tube. This had a one-way valve to avoid the possibility of breathing in through it. The cloth was issued treated with ammonia, which could neutralise chlorine gas. The ammonia would evaporate, so the soldiers would have to soak it in urine to replenish it. The satchel for the gas hood hangs on the door hinge nearby. Gas hoods could protect against chlorine and phosgene gases, but the more sophisticated Small Box Respirator was introduced in 1917 for protection against the more problematic mustard gas.

The old sergeant wears a goatskin coat of a type nicknamed 'stinkers', because they smelled so much. They were issued during the cold winter months to keep the troops warm and relatively dry. He wears a 'Gor Blimey' cap, which has fold-down ear flaps. Its comfort made it popular among troops, but Staff Officers disliked its casual appearance.

Brodie helmet and PH gas hood sitting on the firestep.

The sergeant keeps warm in a goatskin 'stinker' coat and 'Gor Blimey' cap.

CREATING FEATURES

Door and Basic Revetment

A 6ft door at 1:32 scale is 57.24mm, which is wider than the 50mm depth for the sections. A strip of 1mm balsa wood was cut into seven planks 4.5mm wide, which run the full 50mm depth of the section. Three batons run across, to tie the planks together with two supporting diagonals, which run from the far edge back down to a hinge, supporting the extreme side, furthest from the hinges. Hinge plates were made from 3mm strips of 0.5mm styrene, with some 1mm styrene rod for the hinges. The door handle was made from 0.75mm copper wire, bent so that a 1:32 scale hand could fit into it. The ends of the handle were crafted in 0.5mm styrene. A bolt was made from pieces of 1mm styrene rod, with aluminium foil wrapped around to form its mounting plate.

The back parados wall is mainly revetted with chicken wire, stretched over a wooden frame, to offer some support. This chicken wire is made using an etched sheet made by Eduard; this is hexagonal in shape and half-etched, so that it appears to have the twisting detail often absent. The chicken wire was crumpled before building the frame around it using thin strips of balsa. Photos of trenches show chicken wire between timber frames of all sorts of sizes.

The wicker revetment was an offcut from a piece made for the British wet soil section model (there is an explanation of how it was made in Chapter 5). Having two types of revetment on the same length of section adds to its rickety construction.

Section before painting, showing the balsa door with styrene and metal fittings.

Chicken wire frame on the back parados wall.

The surface of the trench floor was dug a little deeper at the far end, so that one duckboard sinks into water. Having fixed the duckboard in place, acrylic resin was added, coloured with brown acrylic paint in thin translucent layers. Finally a couple of coats of acrylic gloss medium were added, with no paint in it, to give it depth. The duckboards are the tapered joist type (for a fuller explanation, *see* Chapter 3).

Sandbags

Sandbags were usually about 33 × 14in; when filled they would be about 6–7in high. At 1:32 scale, a sandbag should be about 26.3mm long (including neck) and 11.3mm wide. Filled with soil, they will be about 4.7 to 5.6mm high and about 20mm long (plus the neck).

When creating the first three sections, a group of nine sandbags were sculpted in Milliput and silicone moulds made of them. Making further copies

Real sandbags at Hawthorne Trench, Kent. Note that the seam is only on one side and the ends are folded over rather than tied.

of the sandbags in resin, it then became difficult to bed them together satisfactorily. Experiments with other methods revealed a better technique and I now usually make sandbags in FIMO modelling clay, which only hardens when you put it in the oven. It allows you to adjust the bags and bed them together well until you are happy with them. They are then ready for baking.

Useful Tip

FIMO modelling clay will only harden when baked in an oven, so it can be adjusted until you are happy with it.

FIMO sausages are rolled out and cut into sandbag lengths of about 26mm, forming one square end and a more pointed end, where the tied neck would be pulling it together. If you are using FIMO, then you will find that it has grooves cut into its back face. These will help in cutting sausages of the same width. Press the bags into rows, overlapping bags on alternate courses like bricks. Seams can be made with a pair of tweezers, working your way along the bag side. Not every bag needs a seam, as some will be on the back face, out of view, or they could have the seam turned inside (as the manuals instructed them to be). The coarse weave of sackcloth texture can be scratched on with fine pointed tweezers or a needle by running scratches along the length of the bag and then others at 90 degrees.

You can buy Juweela ready-made flexible bags (like teabags), which become hard when soaked in watered-down PVA. These can be stacked how you desire before fixing them with PVA. Being 15 × 10mm, they are really 1:35 scale, so a bit small for 1:32 scale. They come in packs of 50 or 100 and can be purchased from Model Scenery Supplies in the UK.

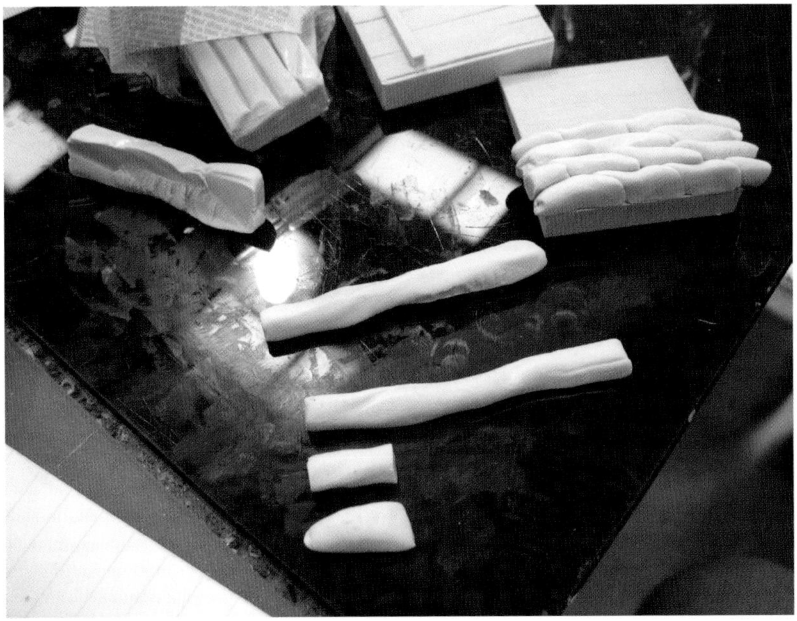

Making sandbags from sausages of FIMO modelling clay.

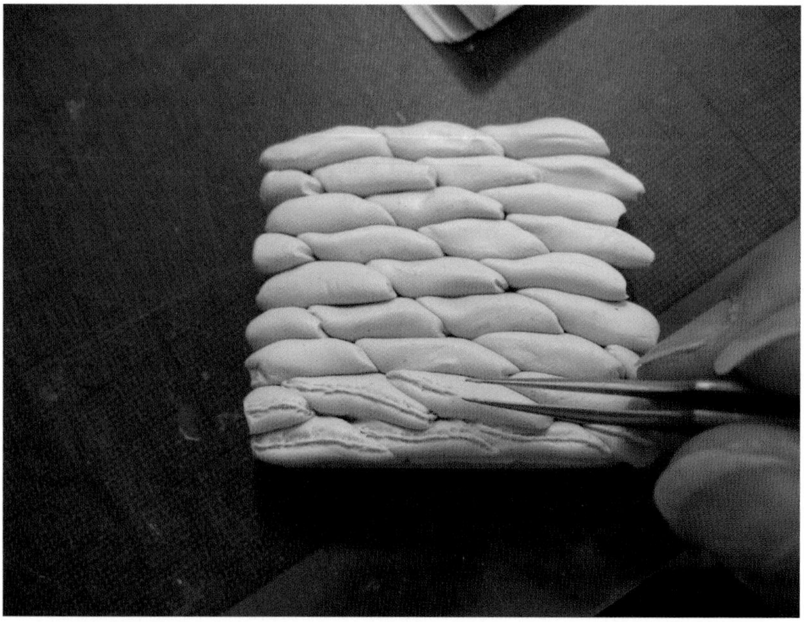

Creating seams with a pair of tweezers.

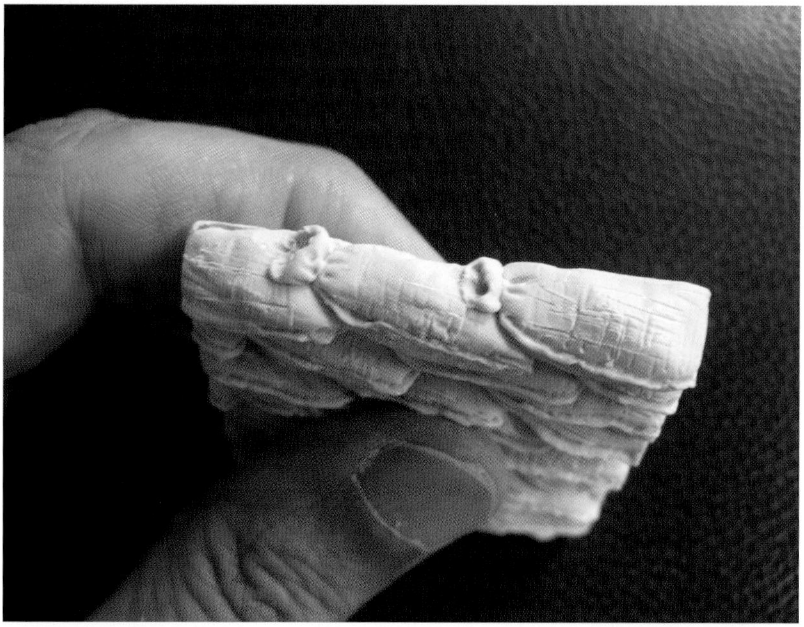

The top row of bags have tied necks showing.

Brodie Helmets

When work started on these section models Tommy's War were only producing figures with early-war cloth caps, so I had to work out a way to make my own Brodies. I have a couple of World War II British helmets, which are similar enough to measure from. They may look round, but they are actually elliptical. A Brodie is 12in (31cm) front to back, 11⅜in (29cm) wide and 4¾in (12cm) high. At 1:32 scale it is 9.7 × 9mm and 3.75mm high. The rim is about 1½in (4cm) wide, which is 1.2mm at 1:32 scale.

A 6.5mm hole was drilled in a small piece of 3mm acrylic and then sanded elliptical, marking front to back where it is widest. Next a piece of 6mm acrylic rod was sanded to make it elliptical and a dome shape was sanded on its end. The rod was inserted into a piece of 9mm tube, which was adjusted so that it was squashed onto the elliptical rod. Once happy with its position, it was glued in place with solvent. The rod was slightly smaller than the hole in the acrylic sheet,

The World War II helmet is basically the same as a Brodie.

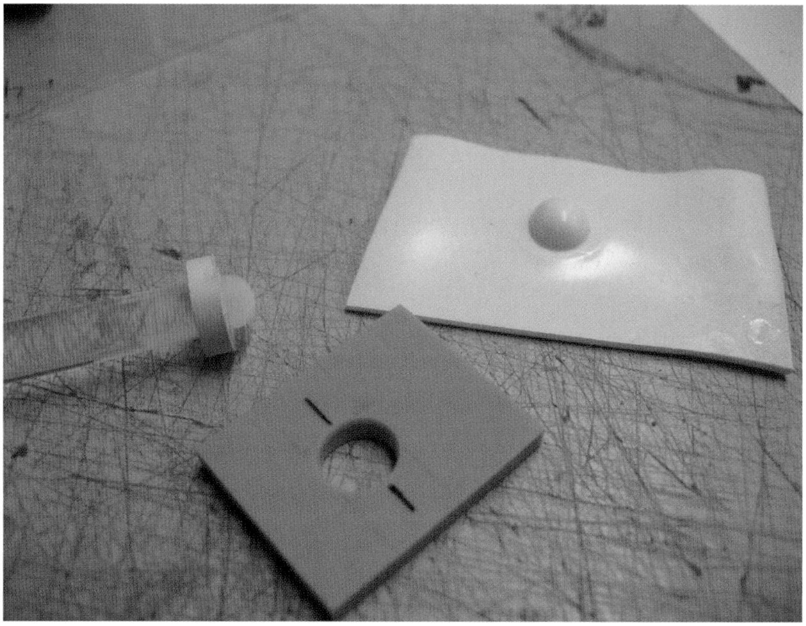

The two halves of the push former for creating Brodies.

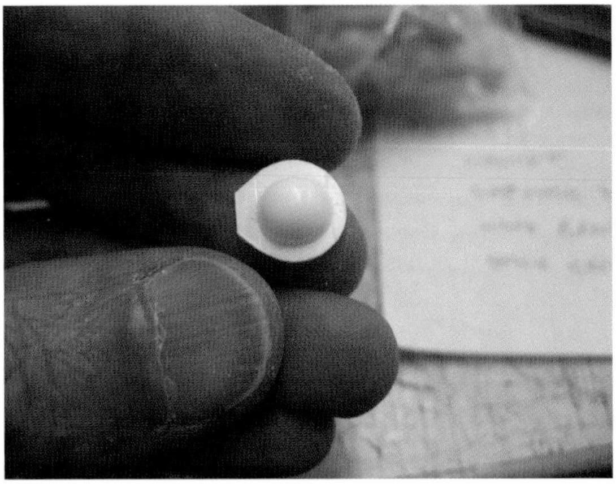

Heat-formed Brodie, waiting to have the rim thinned back.

making two halves of a simple push mould to make helmets. A piece of 1mm styrene sheet, held with pliers, was heated with a hot air gun and, while the styrene was softened, it was placed on the sheet with a hole in it and the rod quickly pushed into the hole. With some experimentation it was possible to gauge how soft the styrene needed to be before putting it into the push mould. When the styrene had cooled the sheet was trimmed roughly, leaving a wide rim around the dome. Cutting the rim back to about 2mm, it was then sanded back to 1.2mm and the top edge scraped to make it thinner and softer. Tommy's War now sell figures wearing Brodies, so you do not have to go through this process, unless you really want to.

PH Gas Hood and Satchel

Gas warfare was introduced in 1916 and was refined as the war progressed. The initial response to chlorine gas was urinating onto a spare sock and breathing through that as urine contains ammonia, which neutralises chlorine. PH hoods were issued soon after and they also protected the eyes against chlorine and phosgene. Gas was originally released from cylinders within the lines and blown towards the enemy trenches by the wind. Later in the war gas could be carried in artillery shells to land in enemy territory, and was not dependent on wind direction. Gas created more fear and debilitation than death, as many eventually recovered from being gassed.

Reproduction PH hood. TOBY DINGLE

The PH hood was made from Magic-Sculpt putty with styrene and wire accessories, using the properties of each material to its best advantage. The eye lenses and a breathing tube were made first from solid materials, knowing that they would hold their shape. Copying a Tommy's War PH hood sculpted by Nino Pizzichemi, it was just replicated using his dimensions. The lenses were 2.5mm styrene discs with wire rims, bent to the same diameter with round-nosed pliers. The rims were superglued to the discs. The breathing tube was just a length of 0.75mm styrene rod, whose end had been squeezed with a pair of flat-nosed pliers. The cloth hood was sculpted working on a piece of polythene, which the putty would not stick to, creating a thin layer of putty with creases and a base hem. Referring to Nino's hood for size, and while the putty was drying, the hard lenses and breathing tube were pressed onto the putty hood without fear of distorting them.

PH hood created with styrene and wire pieces set into Magic Sculpt putty. Dimensions were copied from a Tommy's War head.

USEFUL TIP

Think about creating something using mixed media, exploiting their varied properties to best advantage.

The main body of the PH satchel was made from putty and then given a lead foil strap. The buttons on the bag and strap were made by cutting small discs from the end of a 0.75mm styrene rod.

Periscopes

Several periscopes have been created for these models, making long, hollow boxes of 0.5mm styrene, into which mirrors can be inserted at each end. Periscopes could vary in size but standard models were issued. Some could fold in half for easier transportation and storage. The photo shows folding box periscopes, which are a little more detailed than the one on this section. Thin mirrored film was used to create the angled mirrors at each end.

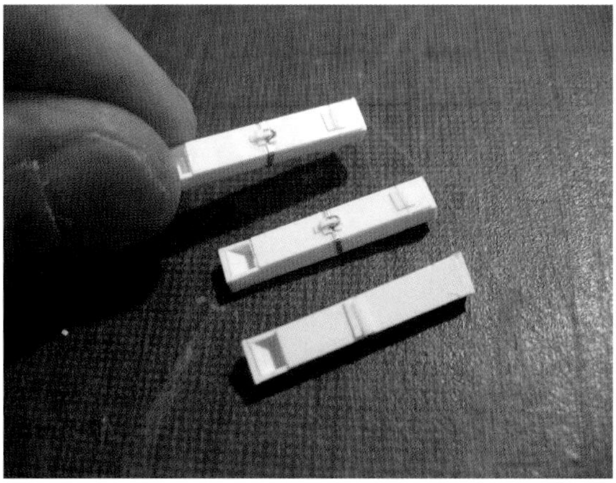

Periscopes created in styrene.

On the battlefield, periscopes would be camouflaged, usually with pieces of sackcloth tied round them, to hide their square silhouette. Nylon cloth, which has a tight weave in it, is suitable for sackcloth, but you can also use plastic teabag cloth (found on some herbal teas), which will take some paint.

STOCK FIGURE

This stock figure from Tommy's War is a Welsh Fusilier from Ploegsteert, Belgium, in the winter of 1915 (TW32013). British soldiers were unable to pronounce the Flemish, so called the town 'Plugstreet'. The sergeant has a wonderful 'walrus' moustache, which was influenced by Old Bill', one of Bruce Bairnsfather's famous cartoon characters. He stands cold and fed up, looking down at new equipment that he resents, but has to use for his own health. His goatskin 'Stinker' makes a change from the usual battledress. You will notice that it is painted a warm 'off white', as it was given filter washes of brown and ochre in different areas and dry-brushed with cream and light grey. Only the final highlighting was done with pure cool white.

The sergeant looks despondently at new equipment, while the periscope has been camouflaged with sack cloth. This is a stock figure from Tommy's War.

Chapter Five

British Wet Soil Trench

This wet soil trench has been dug down to about 3ft below ground but the sub-soil water level has risen and the trench is now flooded. The parapet is a soil mound, piled up mainly above ground level rather than digging down because it is in an area prone to flooding. It only has a shallow parados, for protection from shell blasts behind, because so much soil was needed for the front parapet wall.

It has a thin band of barbed wire hung on screw pickets. The land in front of the soil heap is problematic for the defenders as there is a

British Wet Soil Trench in its display box.

hollow, hidden area in which an attacker could shelter from view. If you look at the section drawing from the *Manual of Fieldworks* (1921), you will notice that the best sighting for the barbed wire is in the 'borrow pit', which would be hidden until you reached it. The parameter of my model is too short to include a borrow pit.

The soldier struggles to move through the mud but has a fixed bayonet as he is expecting a possible attack. On the parapet wall hangs a canvas bucket and there is a galvanized bucket on the parados, which would be used to drain water from the trench floor, throwing it over the parados wall. In the worst cases, water-logged trenches would require draining with water pumps.

A couple of signal flares sit on the firestep, but they would not usually be exposed above the parapet. The rising water has forced a compromise. On the parados are examples of the three main tools used for digging trenches: spades, pickaxes and the personal entrenching tool that every British soldier carried. Water was carried to the front lines in old petrol cans, which were called 'flimsies'.

The soil heap is littered with bits of rubbish, like discarded cigarette packets, a damaged petrol can, broken rum jars and old tin cans. Later in the war, as resources grew scarce, recycling was organized, but there were always discarded, damaged or lost objects thrown about by shell blasts. Rats multiplied and flourished with the chaos caused by trench warfare and here scavenge among the rubbish. Soldiers spoke of rats the size of cats. As they had so much to feed on, they became a constant menace to soldiers, even boldly running over those trying to catch a short rest. If the soldiers killed the rats, their decomposing bodies would add to the stench, so often the troops would try to ignore them. If an area was gassed, the local rat population would be exterminated, but they would soon be replaced by their neighbours. There was no real solution to the rat menace.

Rats scavenge among the debris on the front soil pile. The shell-shattered tree is a garden twig.

BREASTWORK TRENCHES

After the initial battles of 1914, when the Schlieffen Plan had failed to reach Paris and the German army was forced to retreat after the Battle of the Marne, they retired to a long ridge of higher ground called the Chemin des Dames. They formed a defence line along the ridge and dug in to stay there as long as they could, occupying most of Belgium and part of France. This meant that the Germans were predominantly on the higher ground, overlooking the French, British and Belgians. The Allied High Command was extremely keen to keep every inch of unoccupied territory, which meant that Allied trenches were often dug in lower ground into which water would naturally flow. In many areas, particularly those with non-porous clay soil, any attempt to excavate would fill with water. Even if the surface soil is porous, there is always a subsoil water table, which can rise in wet periods and cause the ground to remain sodden. If you dig below this level then the excavation will remain waterlogged, however much you drain it.

The only solution to this problem was to build a trench wall above ground level. If you were in clay soil then you would need a wall of soil at least 80in (202cm) thick to stop a bullet. If you were building a wall above ground, then you would have no soil from a trench excavation, so soil would have to be taken from areas in front and behind the trench line from what were called 'borrow pits'. Trench walls built above ground were called 'breastworks' or 'box' trenches. Often it took so much soil to form the front parapet that the rear parados wall could not be built, leaving a vulnerability to shellfire that fell behind. Although areas of regular shelter would be created, some parts had to be left exposed.

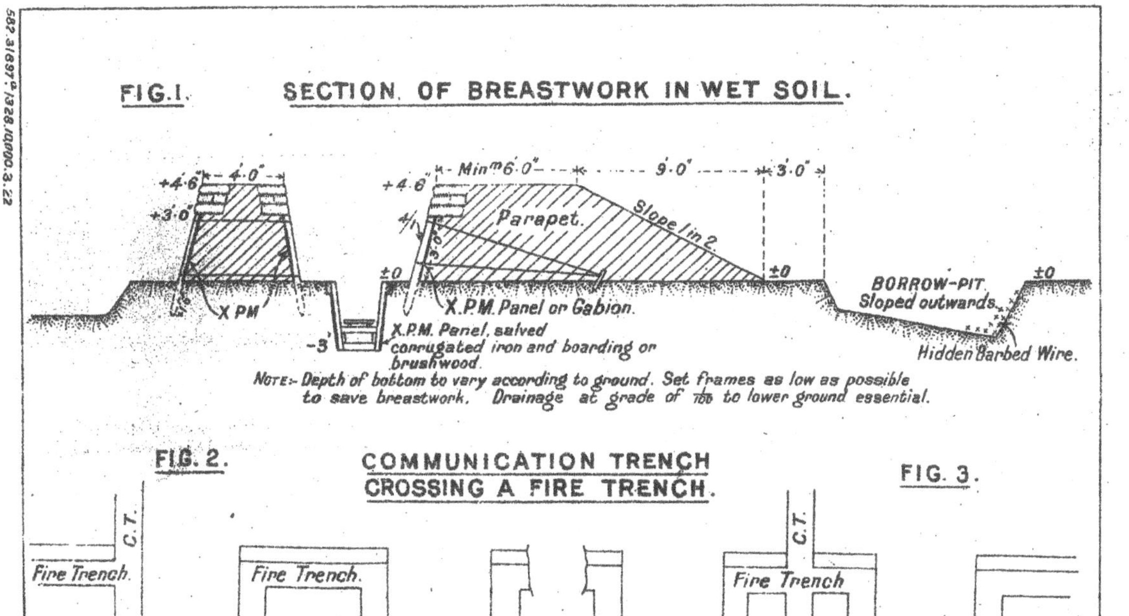

Section drawing of a wet soil trench, from the Manual of Fieldworks (All Arms)*, 1921.*

CREATING THE GROUNDWORK

This section is one of two that had to be made 200mm long (rather than the usual 150mm) to fit the full length of the front soil pile to give a better understanding of how most of this 'trench' is above ground. Being a wet soil trench, much more acrylic resin and acrylic gloss medium was used than usual. You will find a fuller explanation about making wet groundwork in Chapter 2, but on this model an attempt was made to show small streams of water draining from within the soil, down into a gully at the base of the soil pile. Being 'wet', this soil is darker than usual, but the raised parts were dry-brushed with lighter greys and browns after applying the gloss varnishes, creating a more natural mixture of gloss, semi-gloss and matt soil.

The shell-shattered tree is simply a twig from the garden left mostly natural with a few shrapnel scars poked into it and lightly dry-brushed. (Spending so much time in the commercial world of modelmaking makes me cut corners wherever possible.)

There are explanations of how to create screw pickets and barbed wire in Chapter 4, but this longer base gave space to show a simple barbed wire fence with several strands of wire pegged to the ground as well as between posts. The fence is too close to the trench in reality, but was placed as far away as the model permitted.

Grass on this model is made from coconut hair. Occasionally you can buy coconuts unshaven. Once it was glued in tufts with PVA glue I gave it a light wash of olive green acrylic paint. There is a poppy plant among the grass. The laser-cut green leaves are made by the Austrian firm Fredericus-Rex, but I made the flower heads from cigarette paper on wire stems.

On the front soil pile are many discarded and broken items as soldiers would often throw unwanted objects over the parapet; bombardment would also cause things to be thrown in all directions. As no man's land was a dangerous place to venture into, much of the debris would just lie there for years (for information on how to make tin cans, *see* Chapter 7). The broken rum jars are made by Jon Smith Modellbau, as are the two smaller rats (available from Historex Agents). I sculpted the larger rat in Magic-Sculpt. There are several laser-cut paper plants made by Fredericus-Rex (for information on how to use laser-cut plants, *see* Chapter 12).

CREATING FEATURES

Sandbags

The wall of sandbags was made using resin castings stuck together with superglue and filling the gaps between with Milliput. Looking at this wall after the section was complete, the bags are not bedded together well enough, so I sought a better method and now make them with Magic-Sculpt or FIMO (for a fuller explanation, *see* Chapter 4).

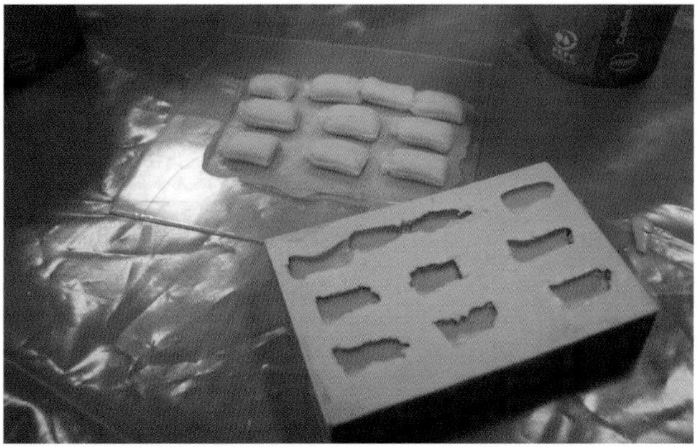

Silicone rubber mould with resin castings of sandbags.

Sandbag wall created with resin castings. Gaps were filled with Milliput.

Wicker Hurdles

The back wall of the trench is revetted with a wicker hurdle, made with woven branches. Hurdles like this have become popular in recent years, used for fencing rather than cladding walls, but made by the same process. This hurdle was made from styrene rod, cut into 60mm lengths. Holes were drilled into a scrap of MDF, spaced about 10mm apart, then 1.2mm styrene rods were inserted about 30mm high with their tops cut at sharp angles. 0.8mm rods were woven between the verticals, which were slightly longer than needed, so that their ends could be trimmed once glued. Each row alternates which side it is woven around and the structure becomes stronger as it gets higher. Once the weaves nearly reached the top of the vertical posts it was painted with solvent to bond them together. At one end a sandwich of flat styrene strips was added to secure the ends together. When the solvent had dried and the structure was firm, it was cut to a 50mm length, which left the extra piece that was used on the typical British trench section (*see* Chapter 4).

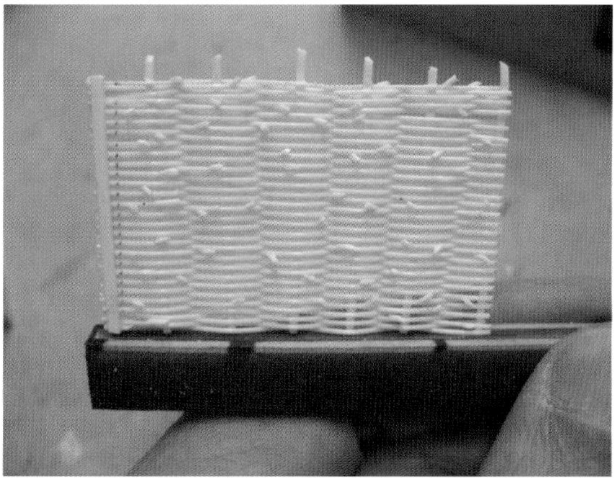

Woven styrene wicker hurdle.

Wicker hurdle found in a garden.

Entrenching Tools

Every British soldier carried on his webbing a basic entrenching tool or 'grubber', which broke down into two parts. The metal spade/pickaxe was usually hung behind from the soldier's belt, in a special bag made to carry it. Its wooden handle with a tapered metal tip was inserted through the central hole of the spade and wedged in place. The wooden handle was usually hung on the left hip, bound to the bayonet scabbard. The dimensions for the entrenching tool were gained by copying Tommy's War accessories, but the handles are usually partially hidden by the soldier's satchel, which hangs over them. The 1mm styrene rod handle was cut to 13mm long, with a 2mm length

Entrenching tools sitting on the parados.

GS spades at Andy Robertshaw's 24 Hour Trench, Surrey.

of 1.2mm rod on one end for the metal tip. The spade was made in two pieces of 0.5mm styrene glued to the tip of the handle. The spade head is 5 × 3.5mm and the pick 1 × 4mm, and their edges were sanded to sharpen them.

The small entrenching tool was there for emergencies, but trenches were mainly dug using spades and pickaxes. Handles were made from 1.2mm styrene rod. Field manuals state that, to scale, a GS spade should be 30.5mm long and a pickaxe 29mm long. The pickaxe was made like the entrenching tool in three pieces, stuck together with solvent. The head has two sides that project out about 6–7mm, made from 1mm styrene. The spade has a 4mm long cross handle on its end and the blade was made from 1mm styrene, bent into a slight curve with fingers and sanded so that its edges are sharp. A 1mm section was cut out of the blade, so that it can sit at an angle to the handle. Aluminium foil was wrapped around the handle so that it looks as if the metal blade wraps around it. This was blended into the styrene with Milliput modelling clay.

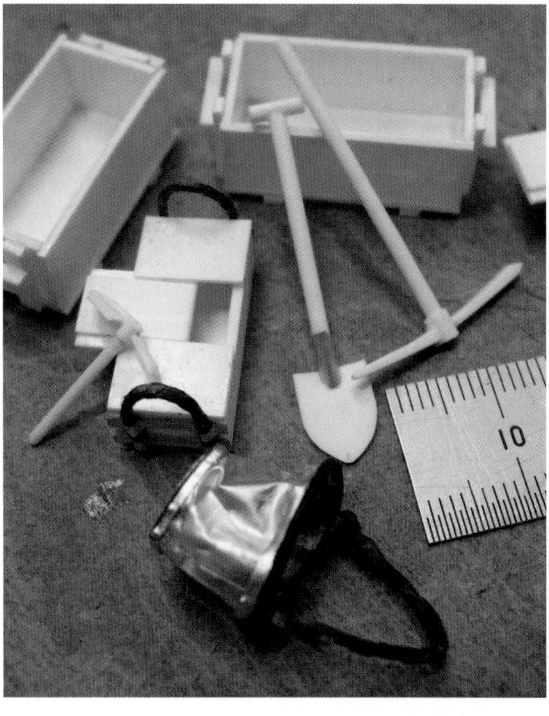

Tools and boxes created in styrene with an aluminium foil 'canvas' bucket.

Flimsies (Petrol Cans)

Petrol cans were nicknamed 'Flimsies' because of their thin tin sides. Once emptied of petrol, many of them were reused to transport 'clean' water to the front lines in manageable loads for a man to carry through trenches. They made the water taste of petrol, but thirsty soldiers, with no alternative, would drink it. They would try to disguise the taste with tea or other flavourings and some even claimed that they could distinguish the taste of differing brands of petrol.

Flimsy (petrol/water can) at Hawthorne Trench, Kent.

Useful Tip

Aluminium foil tape, made for insulation, comes with an adhesive backing and can be used for metal objects because it keeps its form when bent.

World War I Flimsies carried 2 gallons of liquid and came in many colours. They were 10 × 6 × 11in high (not including the handle). Because the handles and spouts stood higher, they were not good for stacking. At 1:32 scale a can will be 8 × 5 × 9mm high (not including the handle or spout). The core of these flimsies was made from low-density polyurethane. The four vertical edges were sanded to round them and then covered with aluminium foil. Because the core is soft, it can be squashed, pierced or bent for damage. The foil is best lightly sanded before cutting it, to help paint to adhere. The base and top were clad with 8 × 5mm pieces of aluminium foil, which comes as a sticky tape. It can be stuck straight onto the core, and then strips of 9mm foil were cut, which can be wrapped around the four sides in one go, with a seam on one long side. Damage to the cans can be created by pressing a finger nail or a soft-edged tool into the foil, because the soft core gives way underneath. You can even pierce holes with a needle or scalpel.

Pie tin foil is a better material for making the handles as it is thicker and a bit more rigid. The handles at 1:32 are 1mm wide and 11mm long. The foil is bent into shape using a simple home-made jig, created from pieces of styrene. The main length of the handle is 5mm, with 2mm upstands and 1mm returns, which fix it to the can. Rather than cutting 11mm lengths, place a long strip into

Flimsies made of polyurethane block covered with aluminium foil.

Finished flimsies.

Petrol can handle jig, which folds pie foil to the right shape.

the jig to bend it and then cut the two 1mm ends afterwards. To get the 1mm lengths, simply put some 1mm styrene against the uprights of the handle as a guide. The handles are superglued onto the cans diagonally, from corner to corner. The spouts are made from styrene discs cut on a home-made guillotine from 2mm and 1.5mm diameter rod. By having two discs, it creates a wider cap on top. (Commercial guillotines are available to buy or you can get cutters designed for cutting matchsticks.)

Cigarette Packets

The miniature cigarette packets were made using paper photocopies. The original flat-packs were drawn two times up, as it was easier and more accurate to work at a larger scale before reducing it. Pencil lines were drawn for 5 × 7 × 2mm boxes. Pictures of World War I cigarette packets found on the internet were reduced and stuck onto the flat-pack drawings, which were then reduced by 50 per cent to create 2.5 × 3.5 × 1mm packets. The edges of each box were carefully cut with a scalpel, using a steel rule. Having got the basic flat shape, they were folded along all the pencil lines using fine tweezers as a guide to fold over. Once all of the edges had creases on them, the main body tab was glued before tucking in the tiny tabs at one end of the packet. Most of these packets have one end left open, as people will rarely close something that they are going to discard. If folding a packet goes wrong, it can be crumpled a little and used as a piece of litter. Into the open end, place a small piece of crushed silver cooking foil and cigarettes made of styrene rod can be added into some of them. Making these tiny cigarette packets is fiddly work that tests your patience and usually requires magnification.

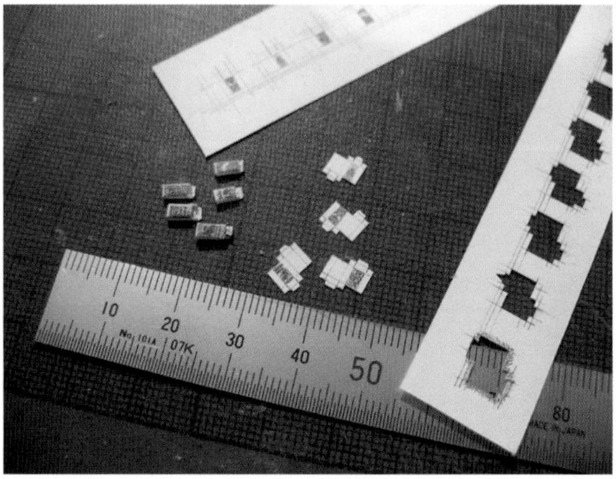

Flat-pack kits for cigarette packets.

Some of the finished cigarette packets.

USEFUL TIP

It is more accurate to draw something small twice up and then reduce it.

CONVERTING THE FIGURE

The figure is another from the Tommy's War range (TW32006), which originally had a cap rather than a helmet. He has also been given a PH hood satchel, as he is now a mid-war figure. The original figure had his gun slung over his back, but his right arm was moved to have him holding the rifle in his hand, using it as a prop to help him move along the flooded trench. His left arm was also moved so that he is grabbing the angle iron post. Thankfully the figure has a strained expression, which helps to portray him struggling through the muddy water. The figure's right foot is ankle deep in the water, so it was cut off with a razor saw and a metal pin inserted into the leg stump. Once the figure was glued in place on the water's surface some concentric ripples were painted, radiating out from his foot. Translucent white paint was made by mixing white acrylic paint with acrylic gloss medium. His other foot, which has just been removed from the water, has water dripping back into the puddle, built up in several coats of acrylic resin.

The figure struggles through muddy water.

Signal flares, canvas bucket and flimsies on the firestep. Grass was made from coconut hair and poppies from cigarette paper.

Chapter Six

Improved Shell Hole

As the war progressed, a greater emphasis was put on building strongpoints, rather than having continuous lines of trenches. Unbroken lines of trenches were easy to distinguish and target, whereas isolated strongpoints could be hidden among the destruction caused by shellfire. The Germans were the first to shelter in camouflaged shell holes during the Somme battles of 1916, while the accurate Allied artillery sent thousands of shells into virtually empty trench lines just a few hundred metres away. The remains of the trench lines could be reoccupied quickly when necessary, but the soldiers could hide in shelters among the debris of battle.

Shell hole model in its display box.

Shell holes were ideal for shelter where trenches had been destroyed or when a heavily shelled area was taken over. It was easier to hastily improve the holes already created by shellfire rather than starting from scratch. The most important thing was getting shelter from high explosive as soon as possible. Several shell holes could be linked together with shallow channels and arranged around a shell hole where a light machine gun was positioned. Some of the craters were designated as sumps, into which water and excrement would be tipped, keeping the manned shell holes as dry and as clean as possible. If the rims of the craters were not disturbed, it would be very hard to distinguish an occupied hollow until you were very close to it. Some shell holes could have small shelters dug into the front wall, hidden from enemy view.

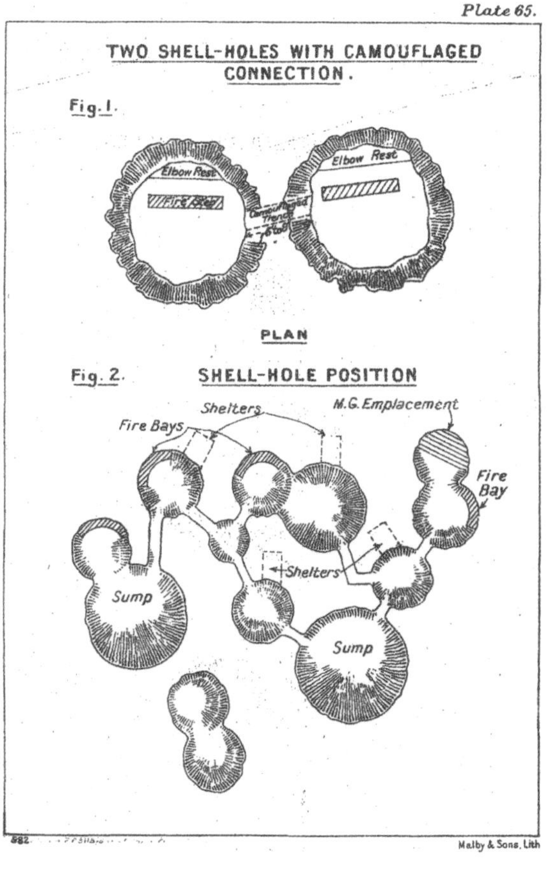

Improved Shell Holes, from the Manual of Fieldworks (All Arms), *1921.*

This section shows a shell hole that has been enlarged and made more habitable. The base of the shell hole is filled with water that has to be drained regularly and the occupants have created a small shelter in the forward wall. A duckboard bridge has been put over the water to give something firm to stand on, and the side wall of the shell hole has a shallow channel connecting it to a neighbouring shell-hole sump. Water would not be thrown over the rim as any visible activity would show the enemy which shell holes were occupied.

Once inside these isolated pockets you could not leave until nightfall or risk being shot or shelled. Soldiers needing the toilet would have to use a bucket or spade and empty it in the sump. Daily tasks would also have to be done in situ, so the soldier sits shaving using his mess tin to carry some soapy water. Water was very scarce, so it would be used for multiple tasks before being thrown away. This soldier must be in a quiet sector, because he has risked taking off his jacket and webbing, while others keep watch. Because soldiers understood that their enemy was just as uncomfortable as they were, some areas began unsigned periods of quiet, which became known as 'live and let live'. The two sides agreed to make each other's lives as bearable as possible and even warned of incoming munitions that they were forced to send by their superiors.

The figure is a New Zealand soldier, especially distinguishable by his 'Lemon Squeezer' hat, hung behind him, but also by his brown shirt, worn by many Kiwis. The figure was painted by New Zealander Mike Butler to look like his great uncle, Percy Munn. He sits on an ammunition box shaving with the remains of coffee in his billy (mess tin), but has stopped shaving because he has just noticed something in his shaving mirror. Percy is watched by a large rat, which were a constant menace to the soldiers, breeding profusely and growing large by eating anything they could find.

The groundwork for this section was built up mostly in the usual fashion, but the curved bowl of the shell hole was blocked out with polyurethane foam before adding a skin of car body filler (*see*

Chapter 2). Dandelions were created using laser-cut leaves and flowers made with cigarette paper (*see* Chapter 13).

CONVERTING THE FIGURE

Because the shell hole is shallow, a seated figure was needed whose low profile would not be exposed to the enemy. Tommy's War produce a stooping artillery crewman (TW32021) with legs bent as he holds an artillery shell. It only required a simple conversion to change him from stooped to seated. (For how to adapt the pose of stock figures, *see* Chapter 8.)

The converted figure compared to the original box art.

As the figure is not wearing his jacket he was shown shaving, although it would have had to be a particularly quiet and safe period to risk removing all his equipment. The main reference for the shaving figure were a few photos showing a re-enactor shaving in Andrew Robertshaw's book *24Hr Trench*, which explains how nearly all of a soldier's daily life was spent in survival rather than going 'over the top' into battle.

The figure and main equipment were painted by Mike, which involved posting them to New Zealand and back. Mike is a fantastic figure painter who does things with paint that I can only dream of doing. Mike paints under magnification and takes photographs, which he studies for flaws and then corrects. He often paints with spots of paint, rather than brushstrokes and paints skin with translucent glazes. Please study the photos and notice details like the hairy arms and even veins on his hands.

The seated figure needed a box for him to sit at a comfortable height. An explanation of how to create wooden boxes will be found in Chapter 9.

Note the textures on the materials, hairy arms and translucent shaving foam.

CREATING FEATURES

1908 Pattern Webbing and Equipment

Because the figure came stripped to his shirt, the missing 1908 pattern webbing was created, using a Tommy's War figure for reference. Measuring the sizes from the figure, the straps were cut from lead foil and superglued together where they crossed over each other. The straps were detailed with copper wire buckles, which were bent using fine-nosed pliers, making sure that they were all the same size by marking the pliers where the wire was bent around. They were stuck to the lead straps with superglue, pressing the straps into the buckles, as if they have a central bar. Ammunition pouches were made of lead foil, wrapped around styrene cores, and were detailed with styrene buttons. The satchel and water bottle were simply spare parts from Tommy's War figures.

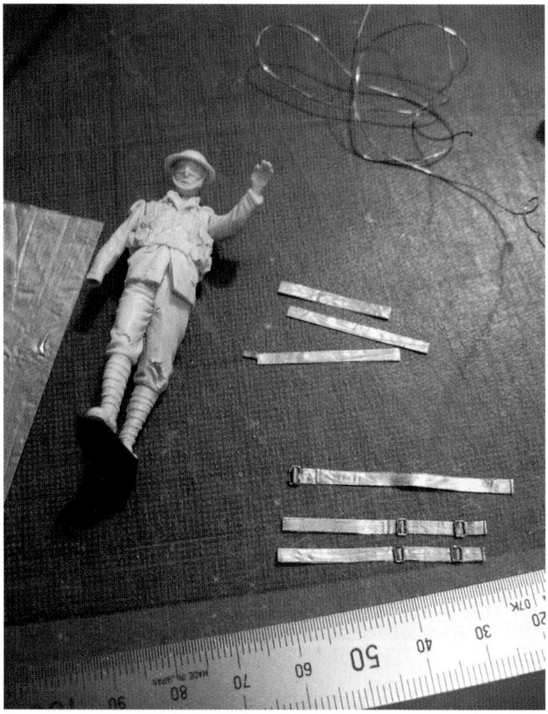

Copying webbing straps from a Tommy's War figure.

Reproduction webbing. TOBY DINGLE

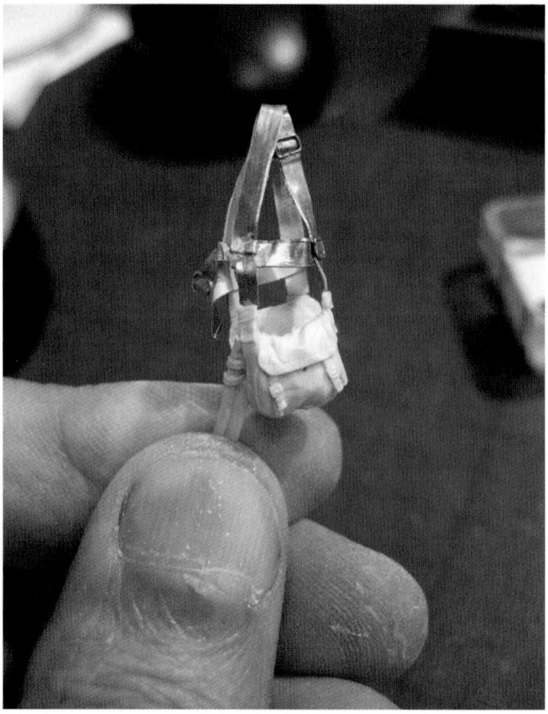

Basic straps with copper wire buckles and resin satchel.

Adding styrene buttons to ammunition pouches created from lead foil wrapped around a styrene core.

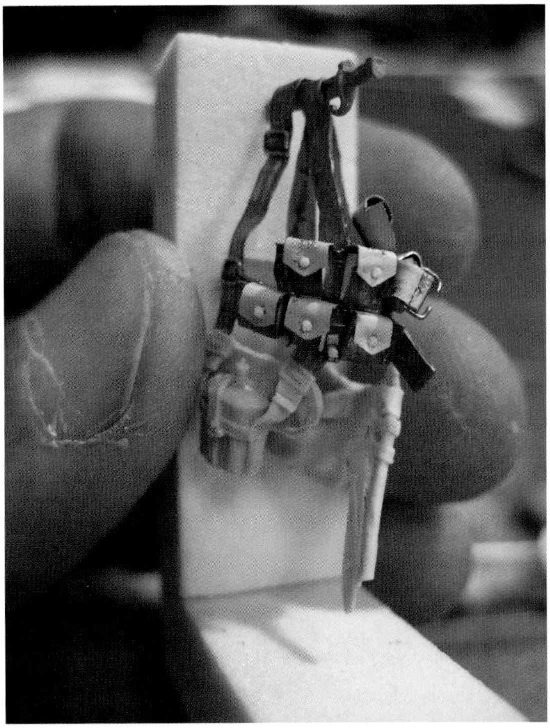

The webbing nearing completion.

1902 SD Tunic

The undressed figure needed a jacket, so again the dimensions were copied from a Tommy's War figure and a jacket sculpted in Magic-Sculpt. To get an idea of how it might hang and fold, the easiest way is to search online for photos of hanging jackets. When sculpting cloth, consider the weight of the cloth. Light materials like cotton will have more folds, whereas heavier cloth like this woollen jacket will have fewer folds in it. Practice makes perfect and the only way to learn it is to try, so make an educated guess as to how it might fold and hang.

Proportions for the jacket were copied from a Tommy's War figure. Note that sculpting should take place on a polythene sheet.

'Lemon Squeezer' Hat

When Mike Butler offered to paint this figure, he was keen to portray him as a Kiwi, so a 'Lemon Squeezer' hat was made from Magic-Sculpt putty to distinguish him as such. (They are nicknamed lemon squeezers because of their similarity to the kitchen tool used to extract juice from citrus fruit.) The crown of the hat was sculpted solid and left to dry. The thin brim was sculpted as a flat disc by rolling out some Magic-Sculpt on a piece of polythene, to which it would not adhere. A wide brim was created and the crown pressed onto it, so that the two parts would bond together before trimming the brim to the correct width. When it was semi-hard, but not quite dry, the hat was carefully peeled from the polythene and the brim was given some gentle undulations. To make it look like a well-used friend, some of the rim edge was frayed for a bit of character. When the Magic-Sculpt had dried, the crown was carefully hollowed with a Dremel burr, slowly grinding out material until the sides became translucent, which showed that it was nearing the outer edge.

New Zealand 'Lemon Squeezer' hat. Memorial Museum Passchendaele 1917.

The figure with his new hat, made from Magic-Sculpt.

USEFUL TIP

Thin layers of putty can be created by working on a surface of nylon, clingfilm or polythene, to which the putty will not bond.

Soldier's Holdall

On the shell rim, in front of the soldier, lays his holdall, containing some of his personal cleaning kit. He has taken out his cut-throat razor and shaving brush, but still inside the holdall are cutlery, a toothbrush and a comb. The spoon and fork are old Historex spare parts, but the knife, toothbrush and comb were carved from pieces of styrene. I have two holdalls, which my grandfather used in

Canada and then during his Great War service, so these were invaluable in creating the 1:32 version. The holdall's cloth cover was made from aluminium foil tape, which was soaked in thinners to remove the glue. It was cut to size, measuring the tools to determine its width. By using foil, the thin flaps could be folded over the tools once they were in place. The central band, which holds them in place, was glued with tiny spots of superglue around the items, as they were fixed in place one by one. The central band and tie ribbons were also made from thin strips of foil. The beauty of foil is that it will bend and hold its shape. This holdall could have been sculpted in Magic-Sculpt, with the tools pressed into it, but the foil is more versatile and safer. The foil was cut to size and wrapped around, without risk of interfering with the tiny tools. There is always more than one way to make things and we all have preferences about how to do it.

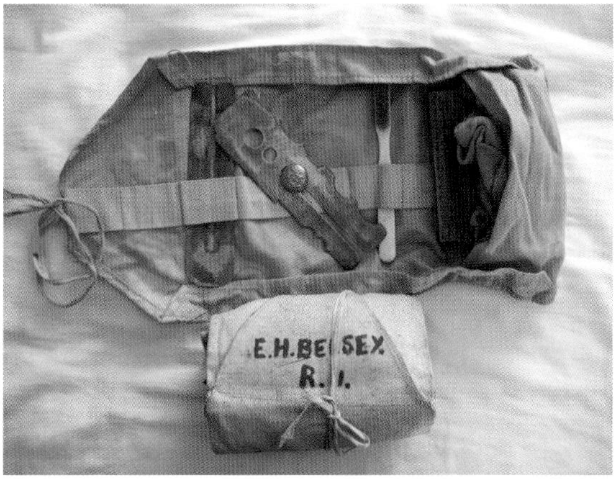

My grandfather's holdalls used during the Great War.

Useful Tip

Use mixed media, creating hard objects first. You can form other materials like putty or foil around them, without altering them.

Shaving Equipment

The cut-throat razor was made of two pieces of styrene strip. A thicker handle section was made from a piece of 0.5 × 1mm styrene about 4mm long, which had its sharp edges scraped off with a scalpel to round them. The blade was made from 0.25 × 0.75mm styrene, which was sanded and scraped on both sides to form the sharp wedge on a long strip before cutting the blade 3mm from the end. It was then fixed to the handle almost at right angles with solvent.

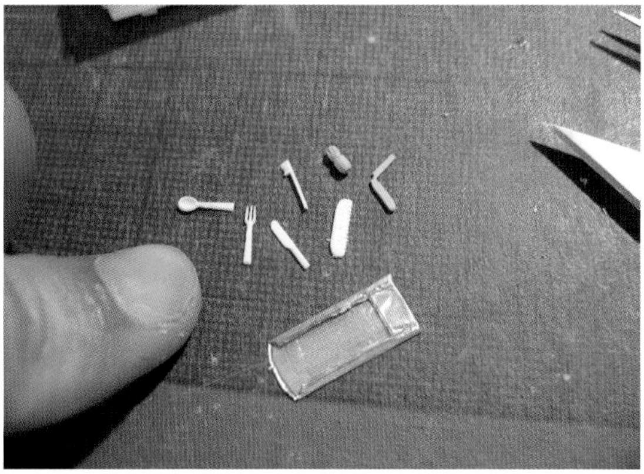

Holdall and cleaning equipment, made from styrene and foil.

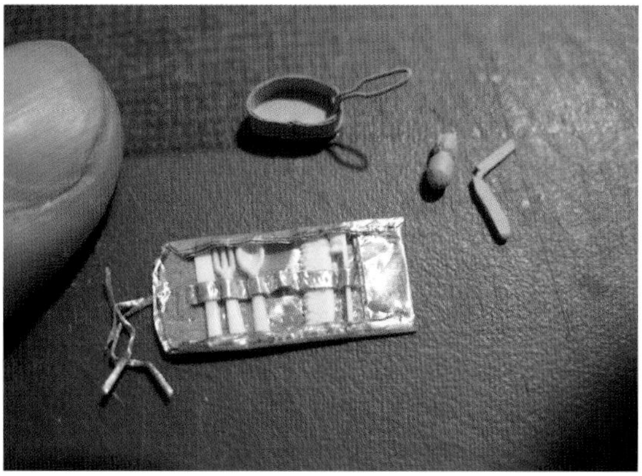

The tools inside the holdall with the billycan and shaving equipment.

The shaving figure and equipment, painted by Mike Butler. Dandelions bring a little colour to the scene.

> **USEFUL TIP**
>
> Invest in a good pair of fine tweezers, which are invaluable for handling small objects.

The shaving brush was carved from 1.5mm styrene rod, rounding the handle end with a sanding stick and then carving the bristles into a soft point, so that the brush fell off the end of the rod that it was carved from. Then using the sharp tip of a scalpel blade, the bristle hairs were scraped into the rod, while holding the handle carefully in the fingers. (Tiny pieces like this, held in tweezers, are likely to 'ping' into the air while doing rough motions like this and the odds of finding them once projected are remote.)

Mess Tin (Billy)

The mess tin, which ANZACs called a 'Billy', was made from a mixture of materials. Its size was guessed but also compared to the silhouette of one that hangs on the back of a Tommy's War pack inside its protective cover. The base was made from 0.5mm styrene sheet, sanding it into a long D shape about 5 × 3mm. Its 2mm-high walls were cut from aluminium foil, using a steel rule and sharp scalpel. Keeping the strip longer than was needed, the wall was glued to the base, starting in the middle of the straight edge and then folding it around as it was fixed. Holding the base firmly against a cutting board, to keep the walls in line with the base, it was glued with small amounts of superglue, added with the tip of an old scalpel blade. This guaranteed the amount of glue that was going into the seam, as there was a great risk that it would simply be glued to the cutting mat. When nearing the full circuit, the wall was cut so that there would be a small overlap to glue together in the middle of the straight edge.

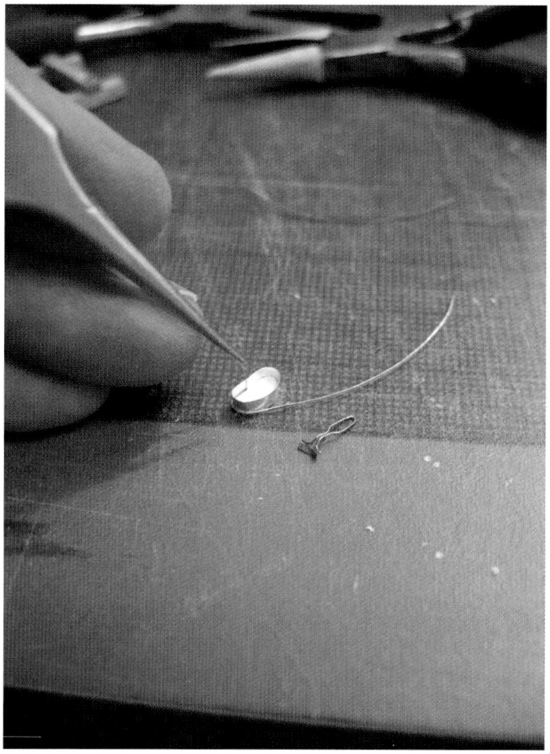

Adding the bottom rim and handle to the billy can.

The Billy has seams on its top and bottom edges, which were created with an extra layer of foil, cut into 0.25mm strips. Again this was glued with tiny spots of superglue, applied with the scalpel tip, using the mat as a guide to keep it in line with the edge. Having completed the bottom seam, the Billy was turned over to repeat the process for the top seam. There was no need for overlap on the seams, so once it was nearing the circuit, the strips were trimmed to their correct length and glued into line. Once the seams were in place, a small amount of superglue was run along the edges of the seams to make sure that they were fixed properly. The Billy's handle was made from 0.25 copper wire, sourced from an old electric flex. The handle is about 5mm long and bent with tweezers, making sure that all its bends were symmetrical before bending the neck where it would be fixed to the inside of the Billy.

Useful Tips

You can usually find photos of what you want to recreate on the internet, but try to find photos of it placed near to something that you can scale it from.

Old electrical equipment is a great source for finding different gauges of useful wire.

Tommy Cooker

On the front shelf, with the figure's shaving mirror leaning against it, is a 'Tommy Cooker'. This was a small, portable stove that could boil a small amount of liquid. The main tin contained a fuel called solidified alcohol. Once its lid was removed, a further section of cylinder with apertures in it was pulled out of the tin to form a platform to put a mug or Billy on. These devices were notoriously ineffective, as they took so long to bring anything to the boil, but they were better than nothing.

The main body of my Tommy Cooker was made from a 2mm length of 3mm styrene tube with a 0.25mm styrene disc added to its base. The seams were added with 0.25mm strips of aluminium foil in the same way that the Billy's seams were

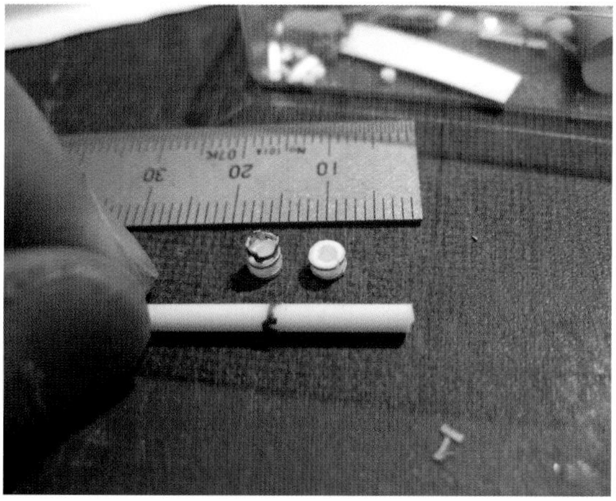

Making a Tommy Cooker.

formed. The extension ring was more complicated to create as it had regular apertures around its circumference. A strip of 1.5mm lead was cut and bent around another length of 3mm styrene to measure its circumference. Bending it flat again, it was then cut to the exact length. This upper ring was made up of three inverted Vs with a central band. Dividing the strip into three equal parts, pencil marks were put where to cut the lead and, using a sharp scalpel, to trim the lead into the complicated shape very carefully with a join in the middle of one of the Vs. The band was removed from the styrene former and superglued where it met to form the ring, and then superglued to the top of the main tin ready for painting.

Rat

When this section was made no commercial rats were available, so I sculpted one from Milliput using reference photos found on the internet. His body was kept low to the ground because it was unlikely that his legs could stand his weight. His tail was a thin sausage of Milliput, rolled out with a finger and then attached to his body. You can now buy beautifully detailed rats made by Jon Smith Modellbau. These digital sculpts are sold in 1:32 scale or 1:16 scale.

Useful Tips

Milliput and Magic-Sculpt are two brands of the same product. These epoxy putties have the same properties and have a similar smell. Both products would be suitable for the tasks shown here.

There are many brands of modelling putty, but they behave in different ways. Some are harder, some dry slowly and all have their advantages. You will have to experiment with them to find which you prefer.

Percy stops shaving as he spots a rat in his mirror which rests against a Tommy Cooker.

Chapter Seven

British Front Line Dugout

Trenches offered some protection from high explosive shells, but shelters and dugouts provided even more. The Germans gained a reputation for building the best and strongest shelters, but all sides resorted to digging for cover underground. British commanders had reservations about troops being caught underground if an attack came suddenly, so they did not encourage digging deep until late in the war, when they had seen how effective German shelters had been.

This dugout represents a small British front line shelter for a pair of officers, built with wood and corrugated iron walls, held in place by wooden beams. The roof is reinforced with a layer of logs

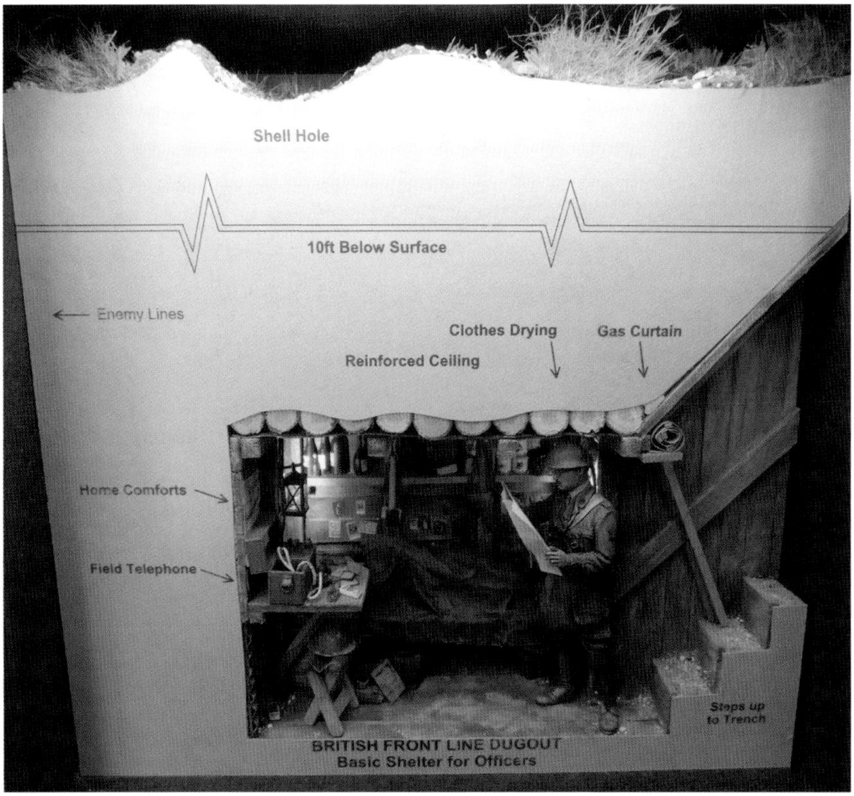

The dugout in its display box.

above the corrugated iron ceiling. The steps lead from a trench above (not shown) and the entrance comes from the front (parapet) wall, so that it is hidden from enemy view and less likely to get a shell landing in its doorway. The officers share one bed, because they would never both be 'off duty', taking turns to grab a rest, if and when they can. The front corner of the room is an office, where they can plan and communicate to their commanders through a field telephone, at a time when many messages were still sent by runners or carrier pigeons.

On the back wall are shelves, stocked with a few luxuries like wine, tinned fruit and meat, along with other things like a football and a souvenir Pickelhaube. Around the walls are pinned photos and postcards, reminders of home (Blighty). Hanging between the shelves is the sleeping officer's revolver with its Sam Browne belt and a trench club. Stealth and quiet were essential for night raids on the enemy's lines, so quiet weapons like clubs were ideal. On the desk is a small pair of wire cutters, used to cut gaps in belts of barbed wire.

On the floor is a copy of the *Wipers Times*, a humorous magazine written and printed by fellow soldiers. Next to it are a box respirator (gas mask) and a pair of binoculars, and near the chest under the foot of the bed is a rat. Rats menaced soldiers wherever they were and would chew through equipment in search of food. Some dugouts had to be abandoned because they were infested by rats, which would even run over resting soldiers when the light went out.

PLANNING THE LAYOUT

The layout of this model was heavily influenced by a life-size recreation at the beginning of a walk-through trench experience formerly in the Imperial War Museum, London. I was very disappointed that the new centenary exhibition does not include anything like this, but fortunately I took lots of reference photos. IWM policy does not allow publication of personal photos, but images of their dugout can be found on the internet.

This model was planned with paper sketches to make the best use of space, as there is only 47mm depth to work with and careful consideration had to made for what would fit in (the sections are 50mm deep including a 3mm back wall). There was little space available to show steps going up

Basic acrylic carcass with car body filler soil.

to the trench above, but it was important to show them. The groundwork is shown above it, to indicate that the shelter is underground, but the labels imply a break, as it would have been much deeper. By putting the office space in front, with the bed at the back, shelves could be put above where home comforts could be added and which the officers would take down with them.

After cutting the basic rectangles of acrylic with a circular saw, the contours and steps were sketched with a permanent marker. A bandsaw was used to cut along all these lines. The outer carcass was built first, before adding the floor, walls and lastly the steps. The groundwork above has a shell hole in it and the top skin was filled with car body filler, creating the circular rim of the shell hole. The shell hole was too big at first and could have damaged the shelter below, so a smaller crater was made by adding more filler. It was made with several batches of curing filler, adding lumps of 'soil' that radiate from the shell hole, thrown up in the explosion. The car body filler is easily sanded flat to blend with the acrylic on the front face (more information may be found in Chapter 2). The whole base was spray primed and base coated in cellulose paint before any cladding or brush painting began.

GROUNDWORK AND CLADDING THE WALLS

The groundwork was painted first, giving the soil several washes of dark brown acrylic to emphasize the textures of the crumbling filler. The dugout is in Somme chalky soil, so real chalk in various sizes was added (*see* Chapter 2). Grass was added using dyed bristles from an old masonry brush, cut into tufts with scissors and glued one tuft at a time with PVA across the groundwork, but leaving some soil exposed where the explosion has burst out. A few pieces of flint, plant root and tall grass were added, and poppies created from cigarette paper with etched foliage.

Most of the dugout was clad with thin balsa wood planks, but the lower areas and ceiling were clad with corrugated iron (*see* Chapter 3). A row of logs reinforce the ceiling, made from a garden twig. The dugout has structural timbers made from balsa, holding up the ceiling. Washes of dark brown and sandy yellow were applied to bring out the balsa's grain, before dry-brushing it with light grey. Extra dark wash was put into the corners to add to the shadows.

The corrugated iron was painted light grey and given dark brown wash, too, before being

The walls have been clad with balsa and aluminium foil.

treated with rust powder made by Deluxe Materials, which is simple to use. A lacquer is painted onto the surface that you want to rust and iron powder is applied onto the wet lacquer. Once dry, it is painted with a chemical that rusts the iron powder. Chalk dust would get everywhere in these underground excavations into solid chalk, so the lower areas, especially the floor, were given a dusting of fine chalk, held in place by acrylic matt medium.

Useful Tip

Fine powders can be fixed in place with acrylic matt medium by painting over the powder or painting the surface, and then sprinkling powder on top.

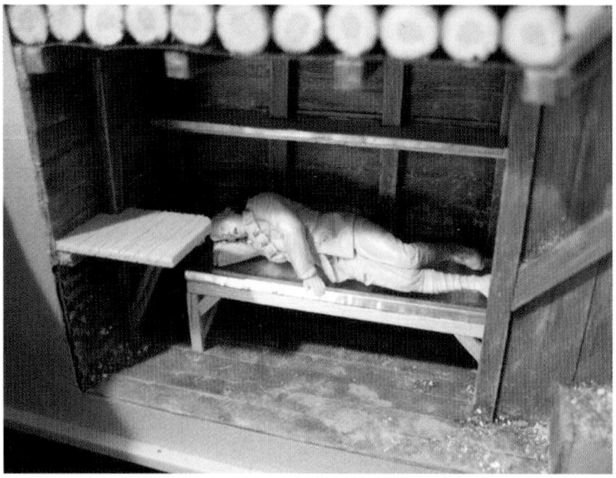

Sleeping officer on his bed. Note the first large shelf, which was replaced.

CREATING FURNITURE AND FEATURES

Furniture

Most of the furniture is also made from balsa wood. There is a basic wooden bed frame with cross braces at each end and a stretched canvas mattress, made from aluminium foil. There was only enough space for part of a desk, but it needed to be large enough to carry a field telephone. The desk position had to be altered from the IWM setting, as that was viewed from one end and this model is viewed from the side. I did not want it to obscure the view. Under it stands a folding stool, made of balsa and metal foil.

Shelves

The first shelf made was too deep and the officers would have repeatedly bumped their heads, so it was replaced with three shallower shelves that sit between the structural timbers. Wood comes in many shades and weathers in different ways, so you will see varied wood colours around the dugout. Great War models can be very bland with their limited palette, so it is best to create variety wherever possible. The shelves and gas curtain timbers were later additions, so are painted a different colour to the wood behind.

There was an empty space at the end of the bed, which was filled with a couple of ammunition boxes made from polyurethane blocks, which were detailed with rope (thick thread) handles, braced with aluminium foil bands. When making accessories like this, I usually look at photos, guess the size and think of appropriate materials to produce it from. Sometimes you can find dimensions on the internet, but it usually requires an educated guess by comparing it to a human figure or something you know the size of. On the boxes are a couple of SRD rum jars. Soldiers were issued a small daily ration of rum, usually in the morning. The jars are digital sculpts made by Jon Smith Modellbau, available from Historex Agents.

Postcards

The wall of the Imperial War Museum display had randomly stuck postcards to remind the occupants of home and better times. The easiest way to make these is to use high quality laser prints. When this project was started I used an old technique of gathering images, cutting them out and mounting them on a single sheet to photocopy. I accumulated a library of helpful images from the internet until the inspiration came to use a word processing program's 'insert image' facility. Much time was wasted reducing individual images to the size needed, but by using 'insert image', in my case in MS Word, you are able to insert numerous images on one page and then adjust them individually to the required size. If you are not quite sure of the size from your screen view, then you have the option to copy it to several sizes on the same page. The first paper images used were a mixture of postcards, photos and a map, which was creased a little to make it look well used.

If you would prefer to buy prints, then companies like ETA Diorama Supplies sell paper prints and Code 533 has .303 ammunition boxes, British Great War maps, postcards and letters.

Home Comforts

The shelves were stacked with home comforts. Historex and Reality in Scale bottles were sprayed dark brown and lacquered before adding paper labels that are just generic images that look like wine bottle labels. It is difficult to view them closely, so why waste time and effort?

Book covers were made by cutting short lengths of aluminium foil, embossed with a blunt scriber and then wrapped around small blocks of styrene, which were slightly slimmer than the cover. One book is shown on its side, revealing pages made by scratching parallel lines in the styrene with the back tip of a scalpel and given a brown wash, which flowed into the scratches. The foil covers were painted black and lightly dry-brushed fawn brown to bring out the embossing detail.

'Warm' LED lights sit behind two lamps, lighting the dark space as many details were hidden, including a visitor below the bed, who was later moved.

Aluminium foil tape. Groves were gently scribed into it for book covers.

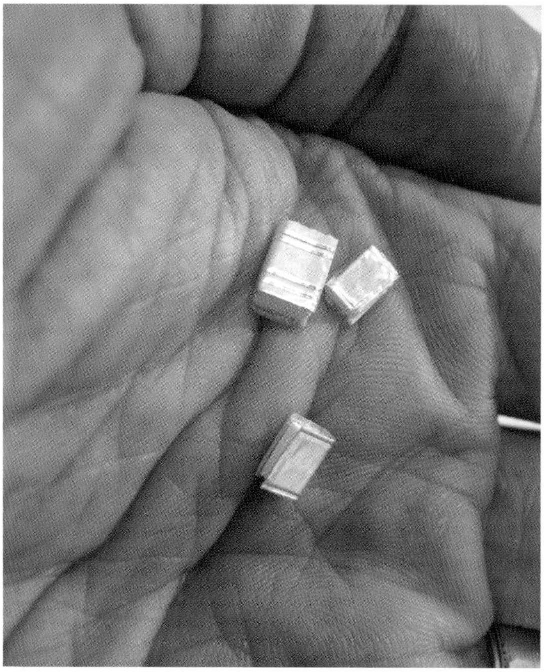

Foil book covers wrapped around styrene blocks, which create their pages.

Tin cans were created from 4mm lengths of 3mm styrene rod. For the rims, copper wire was bent around 3mm styrene rod and, having created a spiral of copper wire, it was carefully slipped off the styrene rod and cut along its length with a scalpel. This created a number of rings, which needed a small tweak to line up the cut ends. The rings were then superglued to each end of the styrene cylinders and sprayed silver. The labels are again generic images that look something like condensed milk, meat or jam labels.

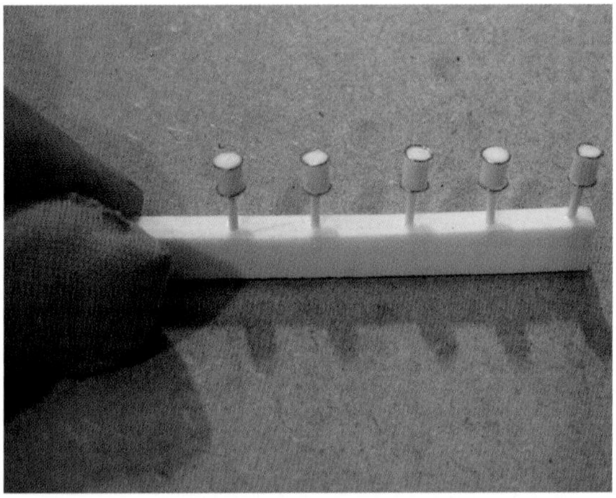

Styrene rod 'tin'cans with wire rims, top and bottom.

Making copper wire rings. Spiralled around 3mm styrene rod, rings were then cut from the coil.

USEFUL TIP

When making things like labels, they are often so small that something that looks right will usually do.

Grandad's Letters

A small personal touch is that on the desk there are copies of some letters, a wedding photo, postcards and envelopes that my grandfather sent to my grandmother during the Great War. The Belsey family have about 200 letters and postcards sent by Grandad, who speaks surprisingly frankly of his experiences. He lived in dugouts for some of his time in Belgium and later in France; one was only 6 × 8ft, into which three men squashed. He had

Reduced copies of my grandfather's Great War letters and postcards.

to tie his blanket around himself at night to stop it falling into the 6in of water on the floor. He talked of making a bed from scraps of wood and having to abandon a dugout that was swarmed by rats. Dugouts gave shelter, but were far from ideal. It is good to be able to include a bit of family history in my models, because this is what drew me initially towards the Great War.

Field Telephone

The main object on the desk is a field telephone, copied from one in the Imperial War Museum. Its size was guessed against the mannequin. The basic box was made from styrene sheet. Strips and then rectangles of styrene were cut using a steel rule and engineer's square. The pieces were stuck with solvent and sanded once dry. Once happy with the box and lid, details were added with small bits of styrene. Studying the photos, an attempt to reproduce something that looked similar was made, having no idea of the function of the dials and knobs. The mouth- and earpieces were made from punched styrene discs, using a pedestal drill and the blunt end of a drill bit. The discs were fixed with solvent to short pieces of styrene rod, which formed a handle between them. The flex was made from thick fuse wire, which could bend into a suitable position. The telephone appears to have a second, single ear- or mouthpiece, which sits in the well in the box. Clasps and straps were made from styrene, foil or copper wire. Experience will tell you what materials to use as it does not matter what it is made from, as long as it takes paint.

Field telephone made in styrene. Discs of varying sizes were stacked to make the headset.

Field telephone. Memorial Museum Passchendaele 1917.

Dirty Clothes

The IWM display also inspired the creation of some dirty clothes hanging out to dry. A pair of long johns, socks and a balaclava were sculpted with Milliput, having figures nearby to check their size. Looking at an actual piece of clothing to see how it hangs or folds will help, but these folds are pure guesswork. The clothes were superglued to short bits of cotton and loop knots were tied on their ends to hang on nails. The socks, being shorter, hang under one of the shelves but the longer items were hung on the end wall, next to the door, where there is more space. They have been painted to look muddy and wet. Wet material is darker, so the socks and long john legs are particularly dark but not glossy, as they are damp rather than very wet.

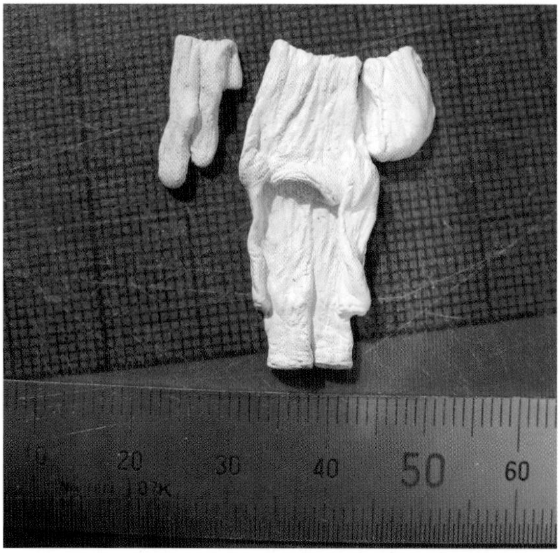

Dirty clothes, hung out to dry, sculpted in Milliput.

Useful Tips

The only way to learn how to sculpt is to practise. Modelling putties all have different qualities and you have to find the right one for your style.

You can make all sorts of useful sanding tools by double-siding sandpaper to small bits of wood or plastic.

Hanging Equipment

Between the shelves, on the upright timbers, hang a trench club and Sam Browne belt with revolver. The Sam Browne was copied from those on Tommy's War officers. Strips of lead foil were cut for the straps and buckles made from copper wire, trying to imagine how a leather belt might hang with the weight of a revolver and a buckle on one end. It was with painted with acrylics, but eventually given a wash of Burnt Sienna oil paint, which gives it a slight sheen. (Always be on the lookout for how to improve things.) The trench club was made from pieces of styrene rod and the head is a slightly wider piece of rod with strips of thin square section on it. A taper was sanded on the handle and a rope lanyard made from twisted electrical flex.

Wire Cutters

Sitting on the table is a pair of wire cutters. Research online revealed photos of a British pair next to a rule, so it was easy to scale them. At 1:32 they reduced to 8.5mm long, made up of fourteen pieces, which required using two pairs of fine tweezers to handle them. The main parts were made from 0.5mm styrene sheet and very fine files were used to create the notches. Eight tiny bolt heads, made from slivers of styrene rod, were gently spiked with the tip of a scalpel and put into small pools of solvent on the cutter head. (Trying to put solvent on the small pieces would only result in them becoming glued to the tweezers.)

Telephone, Grandad's letters, wire cutters and a cigarette packet sit on the desk.

Wipers Times

A friend suggested including a copy of the *Wipers Times* (as British soldiers called Ypres). Scanned copies of the front pages and inner leaves were found on the internet, reduced using 'insert image', as described above, and printed. They were cut out carefully with a sharp scalpel, but creased to make it look well read. The back of the paper is blank, but this is hidden; the edges were painted with fawn paint to dull their whiteness. The magazine was placed in several places before eventually deciding to put it on the floor next to the stool.

An example of the Wipers Times *was downloaded as a word processing document, reduced in size and printed.*

Gas Curtain

The original gas curtain was a piece of aluminium foil hanging down and tied back, but studying the *Manual of Fieldworks* I found drawings for gas curtains with regular batons, which would hold the curtain against a sloping frame and keep gas out. When not in use, this was rolled up to sit on a shelf below the roof. The curtain was replaced with a piece of aluminium foil with balsa batons and it is rolled up ready to be lowered when it is needed. It was made flat and then rolled up. There would be another gas curtain at the top of the stairs, at the dugout entrance, to help prevent gas from seeping down the stairs (*see* the photograph of a dugout entrance at Hawthorne Trench in Chapter 15). The incorrect curtain was another detail that kept bothering me and I was happier once it was corrected.

CONVERTING THE FIGURES

The figures are both small conversions of Tommy's War figures. The sleeping man is modelled as a dead gunner (TW32022), so is not really an officer and wears a SD jacket. The casualty rate among junior officers was much higher than that of ordinary ranks, as soldiers were trained to shoot those in command first to create chaos. Some officers chose to wear SD jackets and puttees, to blend in among the other ranks. Later in the war, officers' jackets were simplified, with rank shown on the shoulders, in an attempt to raise their chances of survival. This figure originally had a right arm that stretched up above his head, but it was changed at elbow and wrist so that it now curls around his head. The woollen blanket was formed from aluminium foil, partly burnished over his body, trying to guess how it might fold and hang. The texture was painted on by Mike Butler.

Aluminium foil blanket, wrapped over the sleeping officer

Note the skin, blanket and cloth textures created with paint by Mike. Notice the gas curtain and angled frame at the base of the stairs.

The second figure is another small adaption of a Tommy's War figure (TW32007). His left pointing arm was adjusted at shoulder, elbow, wrist and fingers to have him holding a folded map. His neck was turned and sanded, so that he looks down at the map. Careful consideration was made where to put this figure to allow the most amount of view into the room. Originally he was going to be using the telephone, but that would block the view from the centre of the room. Putting him near the doorway means that he only blocks the view at one end, where the washing hangs, but not much else. The folded map he holds is a print by ETA Diorama Supplies (Sheet Code 553). I folded and creased it before giving it a wash of Moonstone grey to dull its clean appearance. The wash sank into the folds, helping to accentuate them, and while it was still wet I bent it a little to help it look used.

The figures have been beautifully painted by Mike Butler, who names all his figures. These were named 'Jimmy' and 'Uncle', after two characters from R. C. Sherriff's play *Journey's End*, which is mostly set in a dugout. Mike made Uncle a pair of miniature glasses from bent wire, but also went over both figures cleaning and refining them to a greater degree than I do.

Map-reading officer 'Uncle', adapted from a Tommy's War figure.

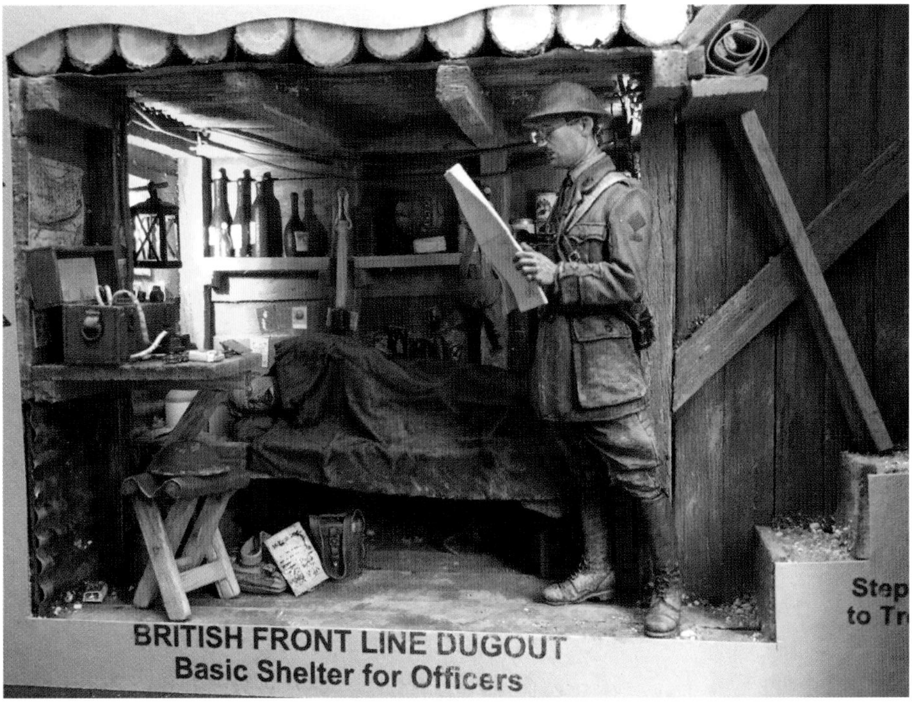

'Uncle' reads a trench map, while 'Jimmy' rests.

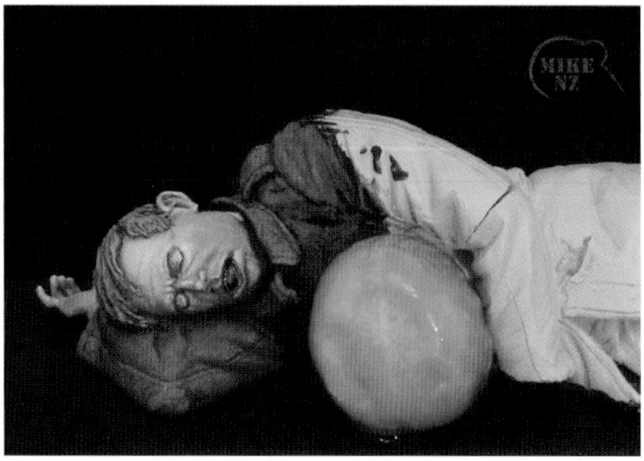

'Jimmy', with Mike Butler's amazing paintwork scaled by a garden pea.

LED LAMPS

When this model was on display at 'Remembering 1916' (*see* the Introduction above) it was difficult to see inside the dugout because it was lit from above, causing shadows inside. I decided to light it with lamps each side, lit by LED bulbs sited on the walls just behind them. A hurricane lamp hangs behind the standing figure, lighting up the dark space one side, while the second is a simple candle in a box frame above the desk. The hurricane lamp was more complicated to build, made with a wire handle and the sections either side of the glass made from punched styrene discs. The glass is a short length of acrylic rod, which was sanded to make it translucent. The sanded surface reflects light so that the whole glass appears to glow. 'Warm' bulbs are used inside the dugout because lamps give off warm light. (Further explanation about using LEDs may be found in Chapter 8.)

A small interior scene, packed with detail.

Chapter Eight

British Tunnel and Mine

The practice of tunnelling and mining was one of the most barbaric aspects of the Great War. The thought that your enemy could be quietly laying explosives underneath you was even worse than the constant fear of being killed by shelling from above. The static nature of trench warfare meant that the armies resorted to classic siege techniques to destroy strongpoints with explosive. Tunnelling

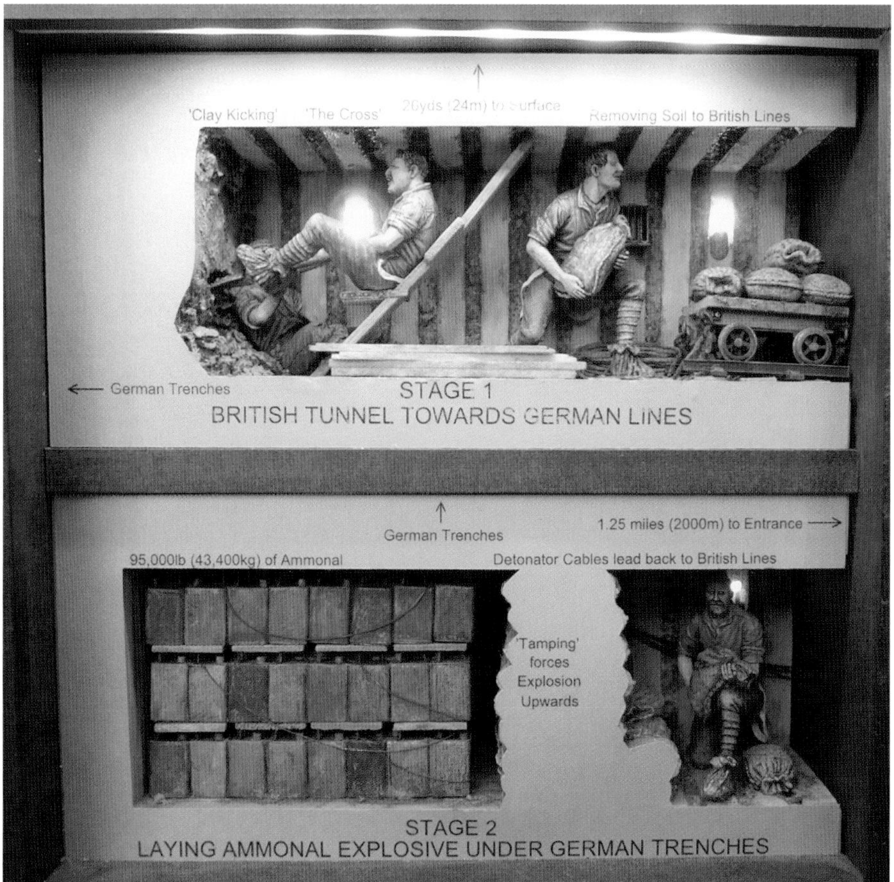

British tunnel and mine in their display box.

was a dangerous, difficult task to quietly excavate under your enemy and detonate your charge before he discovered where you were. Both sides listened for any noise of excavation: if something was heard, a countermine was dug to destroy the enemy tunnel before the charge was ready. The battle developed underground too.

The Germans were first to lay small mines under British Indian trenches in December 1914, but very soon deep, complicated networks of tunnels were dug under no man's land, usually as the prelude for an assault. By mid-1916 the British had about 25,000 trained tunnellers from her empire, organized into companies of the Royal Engineers. Many were coal miners, who were awarded six times an ordinary soldier's pay as an incentive to join this highly dangerous task. Apart from the threat of countermining, the tunnellers were at constant risk of tunnel collapse or underground gases.

The British placed nineteen mines under German lines as a prelude to the Battle of the Somme in 1916. The Lochnagar crater near La Boisselle is the largest scar left today by the Great War. The two charges of the Lochnagar mine created a single crater measuring 220ft (67m) in diameter, and 450ft (137m) across the full extent of the lip. It was detonated ten minutes before the assault, killing about 6,000 Germans. Kitchener's troops, however, were instructed to walk across no man's land and failed to reach the crater before it was occupied by Germans who fought them off.

In 1917 the Battle of Messines was preceded by exploding nineteen massive mines, which were heard in London. About 400 tons of ammonal explosive was used, with the largest single mine

Mine Warfare on the Western Front: exploding a mine under an enemy trench

Exploding a mine. Illustration from Frank A. Mumby, The Great World War: A History, *9 vols (Gresham Publishing Co., 1915–20).* SIMON PARFITT

The Lochnagar Crater, Somme Département. The largest crater from the Great War. PETE BELSEY

about 41 tons. The Battle of Messines was a huge success, capturing a large area of the German lines, but it had taken about two years to dig the tunnels to lay the charges. These were the largest man-made explosions until the dawn of the atomic age, killing about 10,000 Germans. Several mines in Flanders were never detonated. Although one exploded in 1955 during a heavy thunderstorm, three remain underground today, too dangerous to deal with.

Secrecy about tunnels was paramount and many miners (nicknamed 'moles' by other troops) kept quiet about their work until after the war. The entrances were hidden even from friendly troops and their whereabouts kept secret because tunnelling required hours of investment, which could easily be spoilt by one loose tongue or reckless action. They were usually dug from support or reserve lines, with a vertical bore going down as deep as 125ft (38m). In Flanders some of the sandy soil was too unstable for tunnels, so deep shafts, supported by steel tubes, were dug into the firmer clay below. The distinctive blue clay made it very evident that tunnels were being dug, so the spoil was transported well away from the tunnels and hidden from view.

The tunnellers put sacking over their boots to dampen their footsteps, only whispered occasionally and stopped work regularly to listen for the enemy digging towards them. This group are taking a short break to listen for noise that could indicate that Germans are responding. The tunnels could fill with water, so hand or electric pumps would often have to be used to keep the tunnels dry. Tunnelling was a dirty, dangerous and stressful occupation. When the war became more mobile in 1918, the use of mines became impractical because they took months to prepare. Tunnellers were redeployed to dig underground shelters instead.

The tunnelling group stop work to listen for German activity nearby.

'Clay kicking' involved a 'kicker', a 'bagger' and a 'trammer'.

These model sections are based on pen and ink illustrations by Andy Gammon included in *Beneath Flanders Fields: The Tunnellers' War, 1914–18* (The History Press, 2006), which cleverly display cross sections of the tunnelling war. This model had to be split into the two stages of mining and then laying an explosive charge, as there was no way of showing everything in one model.

The top half of the section shows the technique of 'clay kicking', which was developed to dig Manchester sewers before the war. 'Hell Fire Jack' Norton-Griffiths took this quiet method with a group of his specialist miners to Flanders, which has a similar clay soil. The method involved a seated 'kicker', who would quietly push his sharp grafting spade into the front wall of the tunnel, allowing clay to fall gently into the grip of a 'bagger', who would put the excavated soil into sandbags. A third man, called a 'trammer', would place filled bags onto a small rubber-tyred trolley, which ran on rails back up the tunnel. The Germans never developed this technique and continued to pick noisily at their front face, helping the British to detect where they were tunnelling.

CONSTRUCTION AND FEATURES

Supporting Timbers

British tunnellers used sets of supporting timbers that could be added to as the tunnel grew in length. The vertical wall timbers were cut with stepped rebate joints on their ends, which kept the timbers against the walls but also secured the ceiling and floor timbers firmly in place. The model shows a set of timbers, underneath the crucifix chair, waiting to be added when the tunnel gets longer. Freshly positioned timbers in the upper model were painted buff, whereas the older, more weathered wood around the explosive was given a grey-brown wash.

Canary Cage

On the wall is a cage containing a canary, whose demise would warn of harmful gases building up or a shortage of oxygen. The small cage was made with a styrene top and base, using etched brass for the bars. The canary was sculpted in Magic-Sculpt, based on photos found on the internet, but it is only 4mm long and hidden within the bars, so not much effort was put into a perfect result.

Ammonal Charge

The lower half of the model shows an ammonal explosive charge, which has been laid under the German lines ready for detonation. The chamber for the charge would be dug at right angles to the tunnel and a series of sandbag walls were built to block or 'tamp' the tunnel, forcing the explosion up to the surface rather than just back along the tunnel. The ammonal explosive has been put in petrol cans to provide small, manageable loads that could be carried along the narrow tunnels. Detonator wires run past the tamping being laid and back up the tunnel, to be blown from the safety of the British lines. On the model the charge pile has been brought forward to emphasize its size, whereas in reality it would be kept around the corner because the refilled corner space would create the first firm barrier to force the explosion upwards to the German trenches.

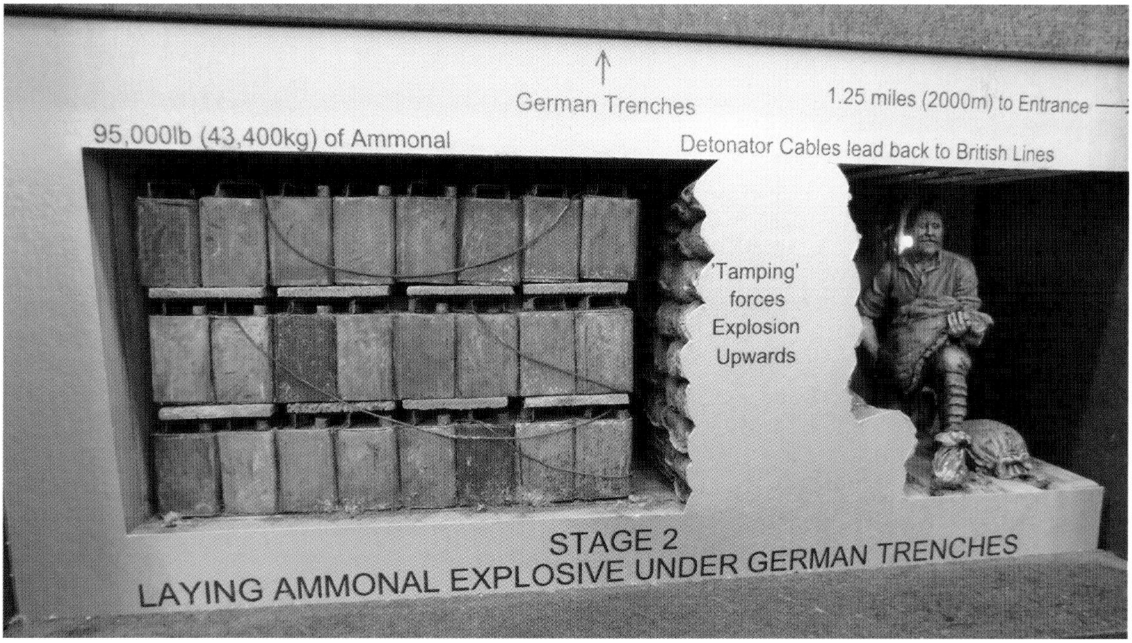

Cans filled with ammonal explosive. Note the detonator cables, which run back up the tunnel to the British lines.

Be Prepared to Correct Mistakes

When these models were started I had no measurements and calculated that the tunnels were about 4ft high. After cladding the walls with timbers, however, I converted a figure to a kneeling position and discovered that it needed about 5ft to keep his back vertical. A fundamental mistake like this would continue to frustrate me, so I had to break the model apart and remake all the supporting timbers. The balsa cladding, the floor and ceiling were removed so that 5mm could be shaved off the top and bottom edges of the front with a Dremel to give the extra height of tunnel. I was able to keep the end wall of the tunnel intact, adding extra filler to the top and bottom edges, while 5mm styrene strips were added to the back wall before gluing on a new floor and ceiling further apart. It was a painful but important process, going backwards, but worth all the effort to give tunnels that would accommodate kneeling figures.

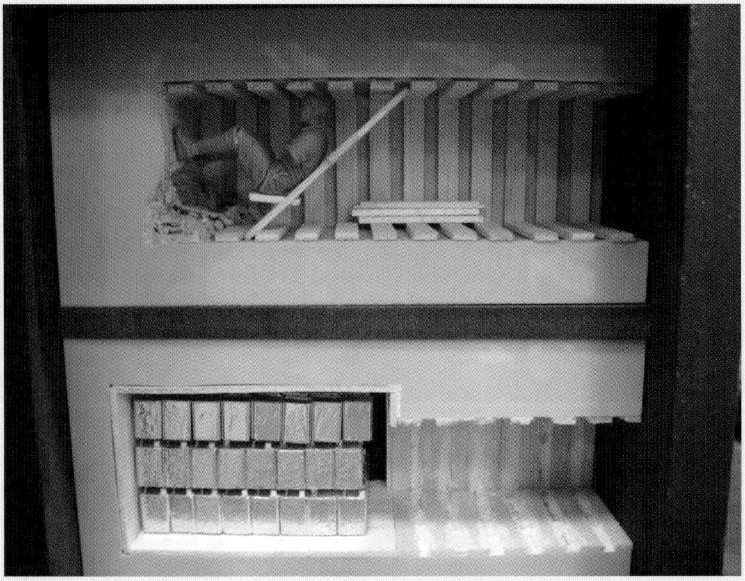

The model with 4ft high tunnels, which had to be enlarged to accommodate kneeling figures.

Blue Clay Soil

The gaps between the timbers were filled with dry Polyfilla because car body filler sets too quickly. Polyfilla, added with a thin spatula and strips of styrene, gave time to carefully add the soil, without getting too much on the wood. The front wall of soil, where the clay kicker is working, was created in small areas of curing car body filler. Some of the crumbled lumps that had gone hard quickly were added as lumps of soil on the floor, glued in place with PVA. Mig textured paint was also added in some areas as a dark base, onto which the distinctive Flanders blue grey clay (similar to RAF blue) was highlighted. The soil was brush-painted carefully between the timbers, before adding dark blue-grey wash. Finally it was dry-brushed and stippled with light grey to show texture, and gloss medium added to make it look damp.

The tunnel end created with curing car body filler.

Crucifix Chair

The crucifix chair had a crossbeam to give extra support to the clay kicker's shoulders. The chair was wedged in the gaps between the supporting timbers and could be moved forward as the tunnel grew, about 9in at a time. The rebate joint was carefully carved in the balsa with a scalpel and finished off with a thin sandpaper file. Depending on which area of the front wall was being excavated, the seat could be raised or lowered. The metal band holding it onto the back was modelled using pie-tin foil with nail heads made from styrene rod slivers.

Carving the rebate joint for the crucifix chair.

Useful Tips

Sanding files of any size can be made by fixing sandpaper to small pieces of plastic or wood with double-sided tape.

Grafting Spade

Illustrations of a grafting spade can be found on the internet. It had a square tapered blade with a crossbar at the base of its shaft to enable it to be pushed deeper into the soil. It was made the same length as a general service spade: 30.5mm, equivalent to 3ft 2in. The D shaft handle was made by cutting about 6mm centrally through the end of the 1.5mm rod and the two halves bent apart gently to form a Y shape. The two halves were then bent parallel, but further apart, with a pair of thin-nosed pliers before a 4mm length of 1.2mm rod was inserted to form the handle. The sharp edges of the handle area were scraped and rounded off, while the other end of the shaft was bent where the blade attaches. The blade was made about 7 × 8mm from 0.5mm styrene. A socket was cut in one end to insert the shaft into the handle and the two sides tapered so that the square tip was about 4mm wide. The sides were carefully bent into a gentle curve with fingers, before sanding the back face to give it sharp edges. The crossbar was added with two short pieces of 1mm rod and the handle was blended into the blade with Magic-Sculpt.

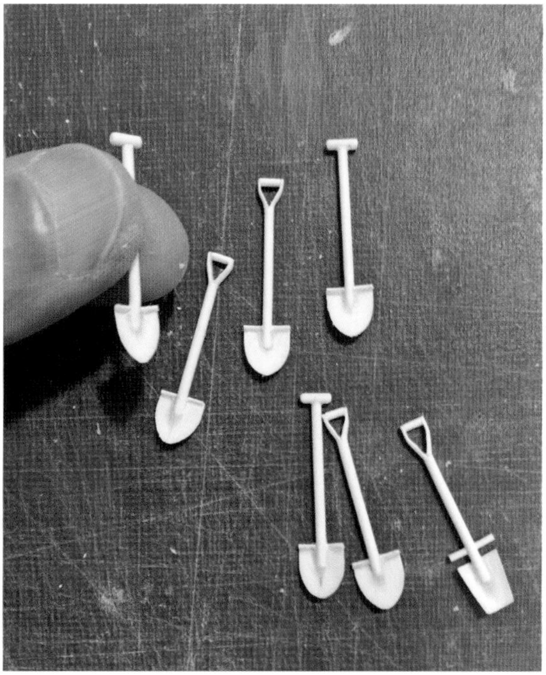

GS spades. The grafting spade (bottom right) has a square blade and a crossbar.

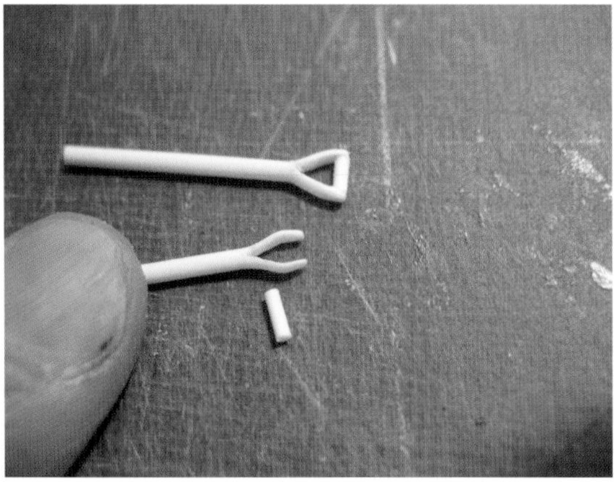

Making D shaft spade handles.

Trolley

This type of trolley ran on sections of narrow-gauge rail, which could be added to as the tunnel grew. The 8mm-diameter spoked wheels were laser cut in 0.5mm acrylic from my own CAD drawing. The hubs and rims were added in styrene, as were all the other metal parts of the chassis and rails. They were spray-painted brown black before being dry-brushed with silver and fawn acrylic paint. The deck was made using balsa wood and sandbags sculpted from Magic-Sculpt. Rings of soft solder were formed around a 3mm styrene rod, as it can be easily cut and bent into shape. A coil of rope was made from twisted wire, sourced from a fine electric cable. After stripping off the plastic sheath with a scalpel, the fine wires were placed in an electric drill and the other end held between fingers to carefully twist them together. To keep the twist together, it was coated with superglue before being spray-painted with primer.

Petrol Cans (Flimsies)

A large number of petrol cans were required for this model, but those in the middle would never be seen so the central areas of the lower layers were made of one solid block. Can-sized blocks were added to the sides that could be seen and foil tape was added only on the surfaces on view. The top layer had more chance of being seen, so individual foam blocks were glued together but clad with one piece of foil burnished onto the top surface. Only the front row was made as individual cans with foil on all their faces. The handles were made from pie-tin foil using a jig that bent the 1.5mm strips into shape, and the spouts were made of short lengths of styrene rod, cut with a guillotine. The Flimsies' handles and spouts made them unstable for stacking, so they required a layer of boards (wide enough to span two rows of cans) between to give some stability. Thin balsa planks were added between the layers. (For a description of how to make Flimsies, *see* Chapter 5.)

The trolley with a coiled rope, a water pump hose and a canary cage.

Foam core petrol cans clad with aluminium foil tape. Notice the solid cores, which are never seen.

Once the adhesive foil tape was in place the individual cans could be marked.

Only the front row of the top layer were made as individual cans.

Completed stack of cans with spouts and handles.

Tamping

A wall of sandbags is being added to by a figure who is placing another bag on the increasing wall. The tunnel would be blocked by several walls of bags further back, as the pockets of air between would help block the passage and make sure that the force of the explosion destroyed the stronghold above. Before gluing the bags in place, some thin electrical wires were added as detonator cables that run back up the tunnel to the British lines, from where the charge could be safely detonated. (For information on how to make sandbags, *see* Chapter 4).

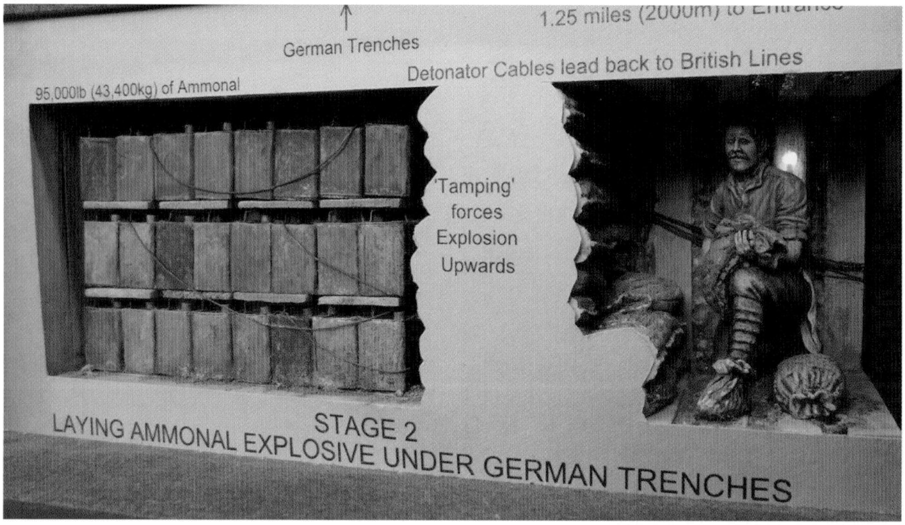

Blocking the tunnel with rows of sandbags to force the explosion up to the German trenches above.

LED Lighting

The tunnels were lit internally using warm LEDs, hidden within the rear walls. Candles were made of styrene rod with translucent orange paper 'flames' that glow when the bulbs are lit. (For further information about using LEDs, *see* Chapter 12.)

Testing the converted figures for fitting. Their limbs have been adjusted but not repaired with putty.

CONVERTING FIGURES AND KEEPING THEM ANATOMICALLY CORRECT

As you convert figures a basic understanding of anatomy and how the body works is helpful, so that as you adjust limbs they stay the correct length. The main structure of our body is the skeleton, which the muscles react upon, so the way bones move is the most important factor. Resin figures can be altered by cutting through joints with a razor saw and then superglued into an altered position. If you are converting a limb to a tighter bend, a wedge of resin can be sanded off but if you are straightening a limb it will leave gaps, which need to be filled with modelling putty. Hips are best altered by cutting diagonally from upper hip to groin. Shoulders are particularly difficult, as the shoulder rises with the arm and back, the shoulder will bend sideways. If you are careful about how you adjust limbs, little repair work is needed to make it good again.

The four figures on this section are converted from Tommy's War artillery crew (TW32020 and TW32021; the latter was also used for the shell-hole model). The two figures have both been used twice, but most of their limbs have been altered in numerous places, so you would not immediately recognize them as coming from the same source, even though they are so close. The seated bagging figure was given a replacement Hornet head (H3201) to differentiate him from the same figure next to him, used as the kicker. The bagger was most likely to get covered in soil, so he was given a cloth head covering. His hand is now positioned raised, warning the kicker to stop work and listen for German activity. Between his legs is an open sandbag, being filled, made from Magic-Sculpt modelling clay. All the figures have had sacking added to their boots for stealth and two carry sandbags, which were sculpted after their arms were adjusted so that they would look right. It is to be hoped that experience will bring confidence about how cloth folds. When painting these figures I knew they could only be viewed from one side, so I did not waste time painting some areas that would never be seen. (This was my last model in the series and I was eager to get it finished.)

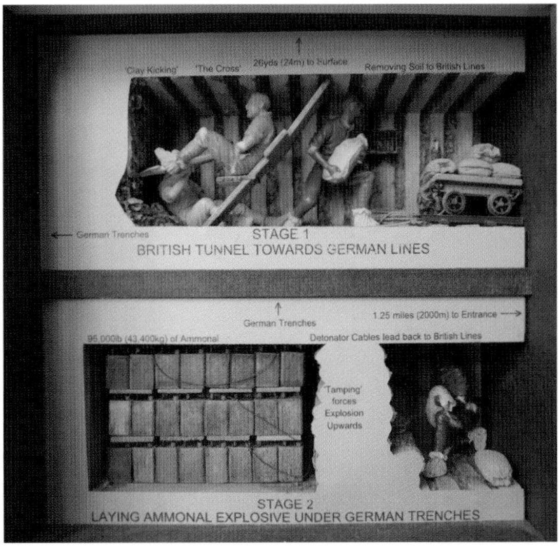

Final test. The figures in place before painting.

Useful Tip

As you convert a figure, consider where the rigid skeleton is and how the muscles work around it. Look in a mirror to see how your body behaves or get a friend to hold the desired pose and photograph them as reference. If something looks odd, then it is usually wrong.

Figures before painting. Two pairs of the same stock figures with converted limbs.

Because both figures have multiple limbs adjustments and one has been given a different head, you would not immediately realize that they are adapted from the same Tommy's War figure.

Chapter Nine

Typical French Trench

The French gained a reputation from the British for poorly built trenches. The French High Command were very keen to regain precious French territory that had been lost in the first few months of the war, and they did not want to invest resources on a front line that they hoped would soon be much further forward. They especially did not want their soldiers to settle down anywhere comfortably, so they did not encourage their soldiers to build good trenches that they might be content to stay in. They also had many more miles of trenches to man, maintain and defend than the tiny British Expeditionary Force in the first years of the war. As the British Army grew, they took over areas previously occupied by the French. Robert Graves, then with the Royal Welch Fusiliers, described French trenches as 'tumble-down' and 'too shallow in many places and without sufficient traverses'.

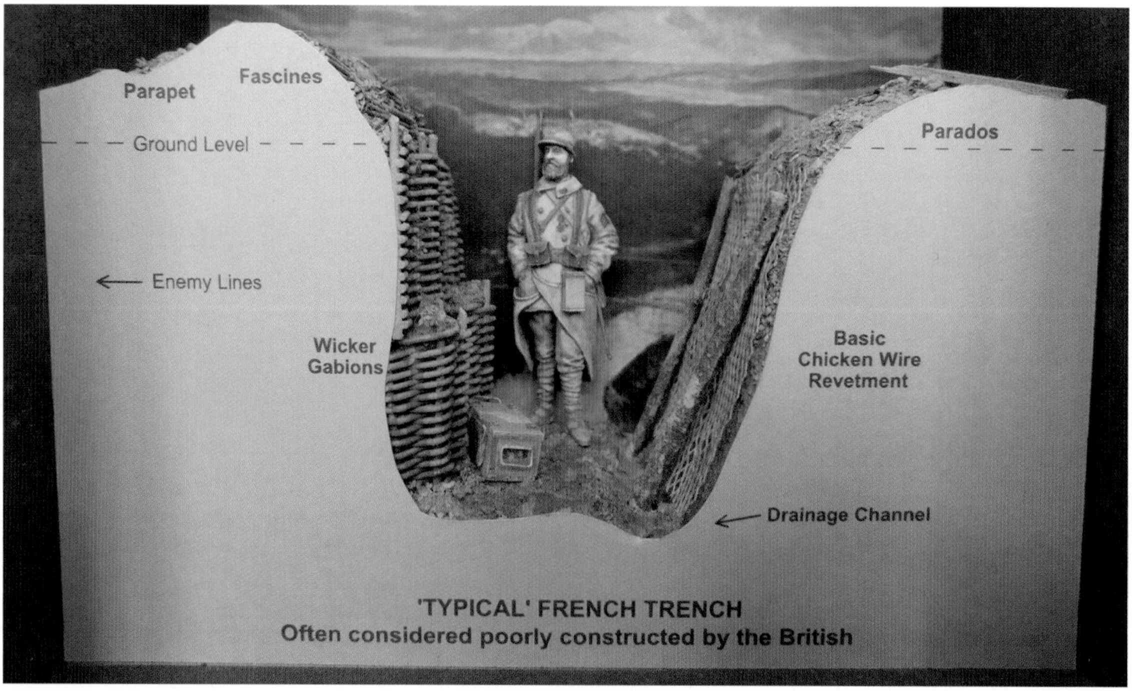

Typical French Trench in its display box.

FIG.2

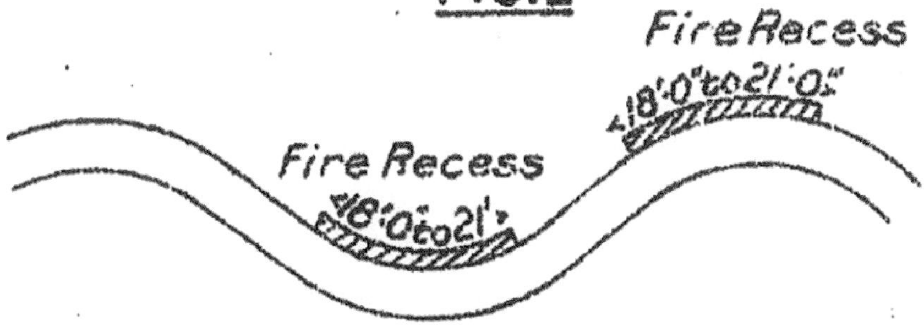

CURVED WITHOUT TRAVERSES

A traversed trench is the better but takes longer to dig

Plan showing curved trenches as the French preferred, from the Manual of Fieldworks, (All Arms), *1921.*

The French took short cuts by not building square traverses, which are stronger and safer, with regular corners to shelter behind from enfilade or shellfire. A typical French trench would simply snake back and forth in a gentle meander or zigzag, which avoided the dangers of a straight trench, but was easier to construct. One type of revetment particularly favoured by the French comprised gabions and fascines, made of woven or tied branches. This model shows gabions and fascines, but also shows weak revetment. As the sections are only 50mm deep they cannot show the lack of traverses.

Gabions are basically bottomless baskets, prepared behind the lines and carried forward. Seven or nine vertical stakes, 3ft in length, were driven into the ground at equidistant lengths around the circumference of a circle about 21in in diameter. Long, thin twigs were woven around the stakes; because they have an uneven number of stakes, the next circuit places the twig on the opposite side of each stake, building strength to its structure. When one twig ends, another is introduced until the weaving reaches near to the top of the stakes. The rigid structure can then be pulled out of the ground and carried into the lines empty before being placed against a trench wall and filled with nearby soil. Being only 3ft tall, you would need two rows of gabions to line a trench wall and they would be placed like rows of bricks with the upper row spanning two lower ones for strength. The upper row would also be set a little further back, so that the weight of the soil in the gabions pulls them against the soil wall.

On top of the gabions are a couple of fascines made of bundles of twigs, bound tightly together, about 8ft in length and 8–12in in diameter. The fascines' purpose was to hold the parapet soil heap in place, in a similar way that rows of sandbags would. Again they were usually prepared behind the lines and carried forward.

Gabion baskets.

Car body filler soil was added that could be sanded smooth.

Although all this effort has been put into the parapet wall, there is no firestep. The soldier has to step onto an old box and onto the lower row of gabions to fire over the parapet. There are no duckboards on the trench floor, so it has muddy

Parados wall made with curing filler.

Dry-fitting the chicken wire revetment.

footprints. The parados (back wall) contrasts with all the work done on the parapet and is basically revetted with a sheet of chicken wire held in place by two branch stakes. A sump channel has been dug at the base of this, to drain some of the rain-water off the path. Despite not being revetted well, the depth of this trench is good and covers the height of a standing man.

The French soldier, known as a *poilu* ('hairy one'), wears a uniform of horizon blue, which offered little camouflage but was an improvement on the dark blue jackets and red trousers in which the French went to war in 1914. Extreme casualty numbers forced the High Command to dress their soldiers in less conspicuous uniforms and horizon blue was a compromise.

CREATING THE REVETMENT

Gabions

The gabions have been made from styrene, using 1.5mm rod for the stakes and 0.75mm, 1mm and 1.2mm rod for weaving to create 'twigs' of varying thicknesses, as in reality. The stakes were placed into holes drilled into a piece of plastic, but not glued. Weaving the thinner rods around the stakes it soon took shape, and when the gabion was ready it was glued together by painting it with solvent, being careful not to allow the solvent to run into the base jig. When dry, it could be pulled out of the holes and a new gabion started using the same jig. Three gabions were woven in this manner and cut in half vertically. Only the front half of the gabions would ever be in view, so the back half, which would never be seen, was not wasted.

Two of the gabions were stuck onto a piece of acrylic, side by side, which was the 50mm width of the sections. Then a second, stepped row was stuck above and slightly stepped back, which meant that there was one whole gabion and two half gabions on the upper row. Smaller pieces of the gabion weaves were cut to create the half gabions on the edges of the top row, cutting them slightly wider than needed. Blocks of polyurethane were cut to fill out their central areas. They were then sanded back to the 50mm depth when they were in place. Polyurethane would not melt when

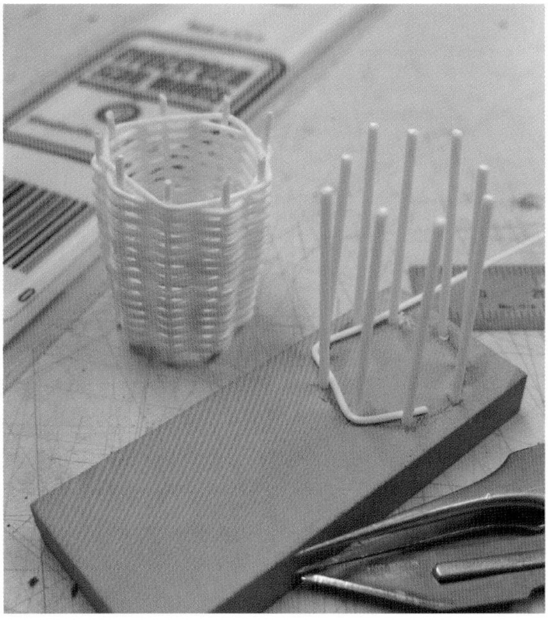

Weaving styrene rod to create a gabion.

Fixing cut-down gabions to a 50mm wide acrylic plate.

coated with car body filler, which is polyurethane resin. (Insulation foam will survive the solvents in resin but expanded polystyrene will just melt.) Some crumbling car filler 'soil' was put in the top of each gabion and between some of the weaves to hide the blocks inside. When the gabions were offered up to their base, it soon became apparent that there was not enough space for them and the trench would be too narrow, so the base had to be put through a bandsaw to cut some more space for them. The sides of the gabions were filled with car body filler, which could be sanded back to blend into the acrylic sides.

Fascines

On top of the gabions are a couple of fascines, made from several widths of styrene rod. The rods were bent randomly before binding them together, so that they did not sit together straight to look like a bundle of uneven twigs. They were bound with wire and a few side branches were added in an attempt to make them look more like branches. These twiggy bits were just wedges of styrene rod, cut and glued on with solvent.

Gabions and fascines fixed to the base carcass.

Painting the Gabions and Revetment

The gabions and fascines were spray-painted with the same Moonstone grey as the surrounding base and they were then covered with the same very dark brown wash as the soil. This picked out the shadows and contrasted all the weaving. Rather than trying to paint them a different colour, a red-brown 'filter' wash was added to the wickerwork to differentiate them from the soil in and around them. They were dry-brushed with the same lighter greys as the soil, which gives the appearance that they have mud on them, but the filter wash makes them look slightly different. The tips of the stakes, where the twigs have been cut at angles, were painted a sandy colour to contrast what would be exposed wood rather than bark.

The parados wall was painted before adding the chicken wire as the soil shows through it. The chicken wire was made from a piece of etched brass mesh, which was buckled randomly before putting it in place. It was spray-painted grey before being given dark brown wash and dry-brushed with the soil colours. A little rust powder made by Deluxe Materials was then added (*see* Chapter 7). The chicken wire is roughly held up by two branch stakes, made from garden twigs.

The base is primed and base-coated with spray paint.

The soil is painted and etched weeds added. The gabions were given a red-brown filter wash and wet footprints put on the trench floor.

Sandstone gravel is added to the texture.

Groundwork

After the car body filler soil had been spray-painted, grit was added to create a more stony soil. A soft sandstone was used because it crumbles easily and has been sieved into bags of differing sized grains. This was fixed among the 'soil' by painting an area with acrylic matt medium and sprinkling the fine grit on top. Acrylic matt medium is a white liquid, which dries clear and matt. When the medium was fully dry and holding the grit firmly in place, it was dry-brushed with several light greys and some dark brown wash added.

My aim has always been to have a soil surface that varies in texture and colour, as it appears in reality. Puddles of water were included on this base using acrylic gloss medium, which had a little paint added to it to make it a translucent yellow brown. Watery footprints were formed along the floor of the trench, making sure that the surrounding soil was darker to contrast with the lighter footprint puddles. Muddy soil is made by painting an area with acrylic gloss medium, but once it has dried the soil is dry-brushed with matt paint in a slightly lighter brown, which makes it look as if the soil is drying on its higher surfaces. The variation between matt and gloss looks more realistic. The sump was partially filled with coloured acrylic resin to represent a puddle in it, but the resin has to be built up in shallow layers because it shrinks back as it dries. It was later painted with coats of gloss medium to give it more depth.

Plant root and etched weeds were added to contrast with the rather dull grey-brown palette. Birch seed pods were used as fallen leaves, and a few bits of clutter add a little interest to the bare soil piles. On the parapet, there is a damaged German helmet, which is a Tommy's War spare part, plus one of my cigarette packets, made from a folded photocopy, and on the parados is a piece of broken timber made from balsa wood.

Useful Tip

A few small objects lying around will make a trench look 'lived in' and give interest to empty areas.

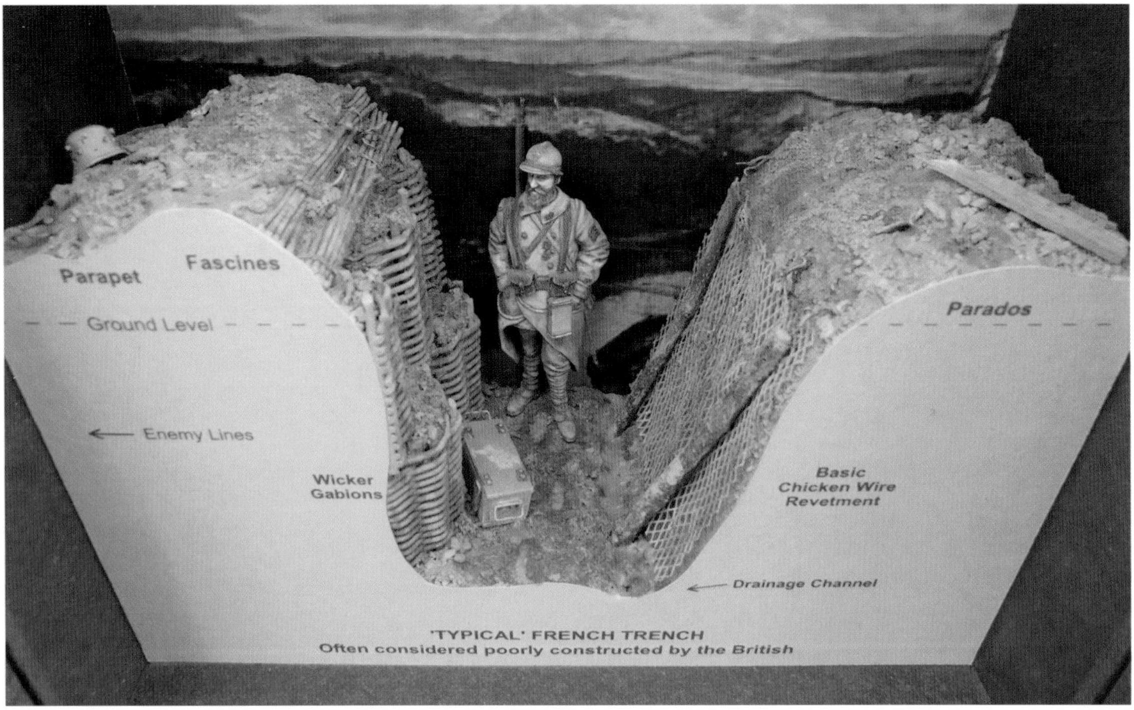

Finished base with muddy footprints and battle debris.

CREATING FEATURES

Wooden Boxes

The inspiration for the balsa box on the trench floor came from a collection of boxes displayed at the 'Remembering 1916' exhibition, where the models were displayed in 2016–17. Creating wooden objects from balsa means that its natural grain can be utilized and brought out with paint washes. The metal furniture, such as handles and spring clips, were made from a mixture of styrene, copper wire and aluminium foil.

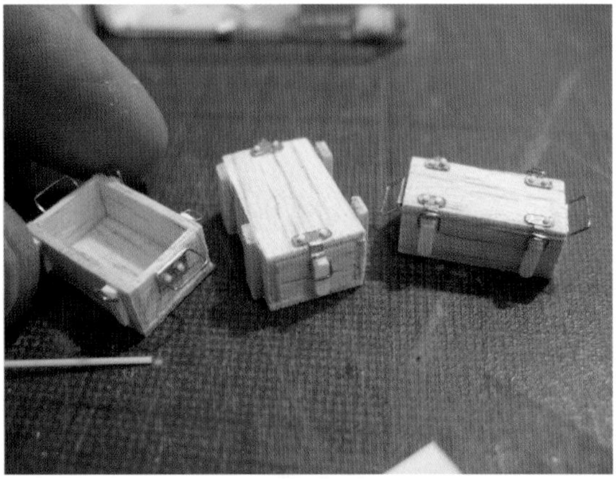

Boxes from balsa with furniture made with styrene, foil and wire.

Rectangular carrying handles were made from 0.25mm copper wire, bent around two pairs of pliers with differing widths, but gave standard lengths to fold the corners around. This meant that both handles could be replicated the same size. The fixing plates for the handles were made from squares of aluminium foil, which was wrapped around one side of the handles and glued onto each end of the box. Fixing bolts were made from small bits of 0.25mm styrene rod by cutting tiny lengths. They were glued to the fixing plates by putting superglue onto the plate and then adding the styrene. If the glue is put where you want the tiny piece of styrene to sit and then put the styrene into the glue, you will have a far greater chance of it staying in place, rather than it just getting stuck

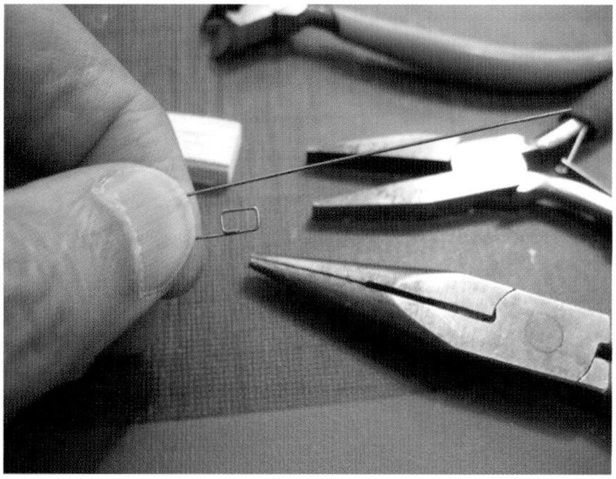

Making handles by bending brass wire around two pairs of pliers.

to your tweezers. You can add further glue on top, once it is in place. The spring clips were made from pieces of 0.5 × 1.5mm styrene cut to about 5mm lengths. The square rings were formed by bending copper wire around tweezers. A small piece of paper tape was placed on the inside face of the tweezers, which taper towards their fine tips. The tape marked where to bend the wire around, so that many squares of the same size could be made accurately rather than guessing.

The box fixed in place and butterfly added.

USEFUL TIP

When making buckles, bend the wire around tweezers or thin pliers to create multiple folds of the same length.

Standard Figure

The French soldier, made by Jon Smith Modellbau (17FI available from Historex Agents), is wearing a uniform of horizon blue and the pose is taken from an actual photograph from 1917. He comes with two head options and I chose the one with a beard. He was not changed apart from adding a bayonet scabbard, which is poking out from under

Jon Smith Modellbau figure on the base.

his satchel. This was just styrene rod, sanded so that it tapers to a fine tip. Jon Smith also sells French spare equipment at 1:32 scale.

Butterflies

The final touch on this section was to add a small blue butterfly, which the soldier is watching. It brings another spot of colour and a break from the dull palette. The butterfly was simply a paper laser print. Searching the internet for 'butterflies' gave identification charts of butterflies, laid out flat. The image was inserted into a Word document, reducing it to a size appropriate for 1:32. Cutting out the print carefully with a scalpel, it only needed the edges and back painted to avoid the stark white and then folding his wings along his abdomen. Sometimes simple things can be effective. All you need is a good laser printer for the quality needed. Laser-cut butterflies are available made by Fredericus-Rex.

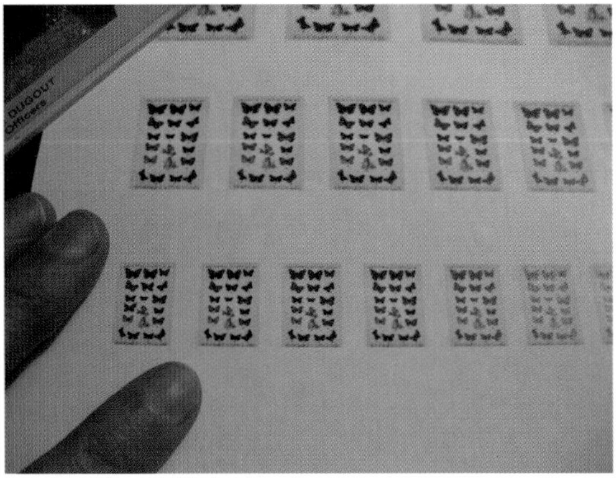

Butterfly prints inserted on a Word document. Note the various sizes.

The painted figure admires his butterfly.

Chapter Ten

Reversed German Trench (now British)

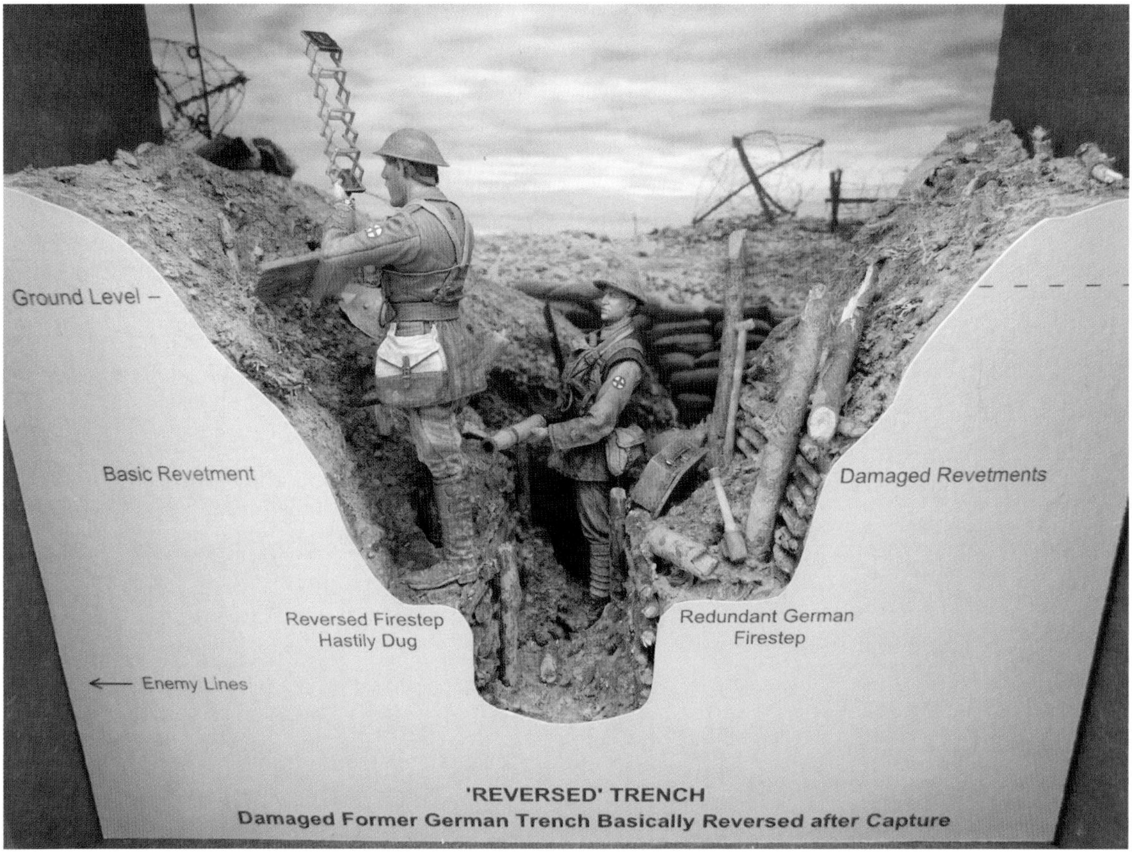

Reversed German trench in its display box.

When a trench was captured, one of the first problems for its new occupants was that the firestep would be on the wrong side, since it had previously been defended from the opposite direction. A new firestep would have to be dug in the old parados wall, which had now become the parapet. This process was called 'reversing' or 'turning' a trench.

This model represents a German trench that has recently been captured by the British. It was usual for a counter-attack to happen soon after territory was lost, as it would be easier to dislodge the new occupants before they had time to secure the position, get their bearings and while they were exhausted from the initial attack. The officer, watching enemy movements though a folding periscope, has spotted danger and shouts instructions to the soldiers under his command.

Drawn by Ralph Cleaver

Consolidating a captured German Trench after the Great Attack: British infantry at work near Hulluch

British soldiers make hasty repairs to a newly captured trench. Illustration from Frank A. Mumby, The Great World War: A History, *9 vols (Gresham Publishing Co., 1915–20).* SIMON PARFITT

This model has badly damaged revetment from the bombardment it had suffered before it was captured, so broken fragments of wood lay around, along with damaged sandbags. The old back wall (parados), which is now a parapet, has had a rough firestep hastily dug into it and basic wooden shuttering tries to stop the soil from gravitating down, but soil is already falling back into the trench. The trench will need a lot of repairs to make it secure once more, but that must wait while the British try to repulse the counter-attack. A British GS spade and Lewis gun ammunition box sit on the old firestep, while the Germans have left behind a helmet and a stick grenade. The British will not touch the grenade as some were left, set to detonate instantly, as booby traps for their unsuspecting finder.

The soldier holds a Lewis light machine gun, which had a huge impact on the battlefield because of its portability. A Lewis gun had a magazine of forty-seven standard .303 rounds, which faced inwards in a pan magazine. The barrel was air cooled under an aluminium shroud, which gave it the wide silhouette. It could fire about 500–600 rounds a minute and weighed about 35lb when fully loaded. The Lewis gunner would be supported by a team of four or five men, who would carry spare parts and more ammunition. As the war progressed, the number of Lewis guns per unit was increased and the Vickers was reassigned to specialist teams because it was much heavier and required more troops to transport it.

The Lewis gunner wears a leather jerkin, which became popular as a better alternative to the animal skins that were previously worn by British and Empire troops in cold weather (the typical British trench figure wears a goatskin). He carries a revolver as a backup weapon, in case his Lewis jams or gets too hot to handle. Both the soldier and officer have lanyards for their revolvers, so that they can be retrieved if dropped.

The officer holds up a Lifeguard Pocket Periscope, which was privately purchased and collapsible, using its 'lazy tong' mechanism. It fitted conveniently into a canvas pouch, which can be seen hanging on the officer's belt. This clever invention was only 13 × 13 and 7cm deep, so it was small enough to be carried without being cumbersome.

When soldiers attacked German trenches they would also carry spades and large objects like duckboards to repair the damage made in its capture. Spades and pickaxes were carried to dig new firesteps, so a trench could be 'turned' or, if damage was extensive, a few shell holes could be linked together quickly.

CREATING A DAMAGED TRENCH

Careful consideration was made about how to show a damaged trench and it was decided to show much of the revetment broken and missing. There is a famous photo of a British soldier guarding a newly captured trench (IWM Q 3990), which shows boards held in place by wooden pegs as a basic measure to stop soil falling back into the trench. This was copied and the damaged timber easily recreated by using balsa, which could be snapped to use natural tears in its grain with little effort.

New parapet with a newly dug damp firestep with wooden shutters that have been hastily hammered into place. The German spade was eventually moved to the German bunker model, to fill an empty corner.

The stakes holding the boards in place have rounded and battered ends to make it look as if they have been quickly hammered into the ground with the back of a spade. This was achieved by pressing a coarse sanding stick onto the stakes and rolling it over its corners. Soil is cascading over the damaged revetment, onto the old firestep and trench floor. Some of the old sandbags castings were used, which were hollowed out with a Dremel burr. On their broken edges some fine nylon netting was added to represent torn sackcloth, and there is soil spilling from the broken sandbag over the remains of the revetment. When it came to painting the soil, damp areas are shown among drier soil, so you will see areas of darker 'wet' soil as well as lighter 'dry' soil. The soil spilling from the broken sandbag is particularly wet and much darker than the surrounding groundwork, as it would have been shielded from the warmth of the sun while hidden inside the intact sandbag. The hollow of the new firestep is painted as 'wet' soil too, as this has been recently dug and would still be damp. Once the soil was painted, numerous pieces of broken twig were added, to show revetment that has been blasted into small pieces.

USEFUL TIP

Balsa will snap with a ragged edge because it has grain. Broken pieces of wood are harder to recreate if you are using plastics.

Old parapet after painting. Note the wet soil spilling out of broken sandbags. Root, weeds and broken pieces of garden twig lie around.

Curing filler was added in small quantities, distinguished by the differing pinks.

A detailed explanation of how I create soil using car body filler will be found in Chapter 2, but you will see from the progress photos of this section how car body filler is laid in small areas of curing filler, noticeable by the varying shades of pink. The more red catalyst you add, the quicker it will cure and become pinker. The pieces of balsa wood and twig were kept loose until after the base was spray-painted, wrapping these pieces in adhesive tape as a release agent before spreading the car body filler around them, so that it would not adhere to them. The pieces needed a gentle tweak to release them once the filler had cured. The tape was then removed and checked that they still fitted into the cavities they had left. (You must not allow the filler to overhang any object or you will not be able to remove it.) Once the bases were primed and base-coated, the wood and twigs were glued in place and any gaps were filled with dry, crumbling Polyfilla.

Base prepared for painting. The wooden pieces are all kept loose until the base is spray-painted.

The items of equipment abandoned by their previous German owners were mostly spare parts by a company called JMD Miniatures, although these are no longer available. The typically German spade would have been hidden behind the officer and was eventually moved to the German bunker model where it could be seen. The British equivalent GS spade and Lewis ammunition tin on the old firestep were scratch-built in styrene. The German helmet was a Tommy's War spare part. You can now buy German spare equipment from Jon Smith Modellbau.

Base-coated in Moonstone grey. The wooden pieces are now stuck in place.

The new firestep with the wood fixed in place after the base coat was sprayed.

The old, broken parapet in its base coat. The wood is now fixed in place.

Gaps behind the revetments are filled with Polyfllla.

The paint and Polyfilla are given a wash of dark brown.

Photo reference for the folding periscope.

Creating the lazy tong mechanism in styrene. Short pieces of styrene strip are cut using a guillotine.

CREATING A FOLDING TELESCOPE

Having found numerous photos of Lifeguard Pocket Periscopes on the internet, a listing by the Imperial War Museum even had its dimensions. The mirrors were 13cm square, which meant that a 1:32 version would be about 4mm square. Two pieces of 0.5mm styrene were cut for these and then several 4mm lengths of 0.25 × 0.5mm styrene were cut to make the lazy tong mechanism. A piece of MDF was marked up with 3mm spacings and some double-sided tape was stuck over this. The small lengths of styrene strip were cut on my home-made guillotine and lightly tacked onto the double-sided tape, which kept them in place until the upper returns were added, glued with tiny drops of solvent to their joints with a fine paintbrush. Eight pairs of tongs were stuck together, but both ends were trimmed off where the mirrors would sit, as these bars were only half the length. Having made one side, the process was then repeated, but mirrored.

When the solvent had dried, the tongs mechanisms were carefully removed by gently putting a scalpel under them. A few joints came loose, but it held its shape enough to repair. The tongs were then glued to the edges of the mirrors at each end and three crossbars were added on each side. Being so small, it was hard to make everything straight, but it was adjusted where it was most obviously wonky. It is not perfect, but good enough for something so small. The mirrors were glued onto the frames once everything was painted and are made from a very thin mirrored film that was found at work.

Useful Tip

If you don't have a guillotine, then cut a master piece to the desired length and mark it as the template. Use this as a guide to cut others of the same length.

CONVERTING FIGURES

Both figures are adapted from the Tommy's War range. The officer figure (TW320G01) comes with an early-war flat cap, which was razor-sawed off to give him a Brodie helmet, pinched from another figure. The helmet was carefully razor-sawed off that figure's head just under the rim, which left part of the head still inside and that had to be removed carefully with a Dremel burr. Once the helmet was glued on to the officer, a foil strap was made for the helmet, which was placed behind his head as soldiers often wore. It has a square buckle made of fine copper wire scavenged from electric flex, which was bent around tweezers.

The only change to his pose was to replace his left hand. The original figure was looking at his watch and holding a swagger stick. As that hand was clenched, a spare one had to be found. Historex Agents sell a set of sixteen pairs of hands and four pairs of bare feet for 54mm figures (Historex Spare Parts 30372). An open hand was used that would accept the folding periscope, so the officer now looks into that rather than his watch. The figure comes with a pouch on the right-hand side of his belt. It was the right width but was a little short. Some Milliput was added to its base to make it 4mm square so that the periscope would fit into it. It was carved under its flap a little so that it looked more open and a trailing foil strap was added, which was a feature of the Lifeguard Periscope pouch. The lanyard to his revolver is copper wire, held together by a toggle on his chest made from a small piece of

Primed figures after adapting the Lewis gunner and adding box respirators.

foil, but this is now covered by his respirator. This officer was originally given a PH hood satchel, but that was later replaced with a sculpted small box respirator bag to match the Lewis gunner, as it is unlikely that an officer would be carrying an older version of respirator than his soldiers. Fine wires were added around the figure's chest to represent the cords that held the respirator in place. The bag strap, also sculpted with Magic-Sculpt, is pulled halfway down his back, holding the respirator on his chest.

The second figure is a Tommy's War's Lewis gunner (TW32029) and he was put on the base virtually unchanged at first, until Mike Butler persuaded me to adapt him further to a pose that he liked in a book. Mike's illustration had a much more youthful face, so I gave him a new Hornet 54mm head (H3202) (available from Historex Agents). The Lewis gunner's Brodie was razor-sawed off and stuck onto the new head, once a little of its crown had been removed. The head was turned round to look towards the officer giving orders and his Lewis gun was replaced with a more detailed gun made by Kellerkind-Miniaturen (available from Sockel and Bases, Germany).

Primed figures on the base. The pose of the Lewis gunner was later changed.

The pose that Mike wanted to recreate meant that the figure would now be carrying the Lewis rather than just resting it on the ground. I naively thought that it would be simple to move his arms forward to carry the gun. Only when I had started to chop him about did I realize that the weight of the gun would actually bring the gun into his belly, so some of his leather jerkin would have to be carved out too. A heavy piece of equipment like a Lewis could not be held out at arm's length as its weight would pull it into the leather and soft tissue of his belly onto his pelvis. The way his right hand grasps the trigger handle is complicated too, because the arm hangs in front of the gun and his hand twists round to grip the handle. More spare hands had to be found to adapt and carve for this pose, sculpting new fingers in Magic-Sculpt to grip the handle firmly. It became more of a task than first realized, but it was worth all the effort, if Mike were to add his magic paintwork. Mike also suggested a few more changes, such as reworking his box respirator. Soldiers would often wear their bags open and backwards, with the hose hanging out, ready to be pulled out quickly if a gas shell landed nearby. The top area of the bag was carved out and a new flap sculpted with Magic-Sculpt, because it was now on the front. The hose was simply made from a bent guitar string (low E2).

These figures were named 'Harry' and 'Bob' after the longest surviving Great War Tommy, Harry Patch (111), who was in the Duke of Cornwall's Light Infantry. He was an assistant Lewis gunner to a Bob Hayes, so Harry has been promoted to

Bob – Mike brings this 54mm figure to life with his extraordinary paintwork.

Harry – Mike has patiently and skillfully painted character as well as realistic skin, cloth textures and mud on this battle weary but determined figure.

No.1 and Bob to an officer. The figure 'Harry' was broken in transit to New Zealand and Mike reworked his hands and arms. Because his painting is to a far higher spec than mine, he also spent hours cleaning and enhancing the figures by creating things like shirt cuffs inside the jackets and helmet liners. It is worth the risk of sending my figures to the opposite side of the world to get Mike's help. Our perfectionism appears in different ways, but we have a great partnership.

After a trip around the world the figures are finally in place in a battle-damaged trench.

The Lewis gunner awaits orders from the shouting officer, who has spotted danger through his folding periscope.

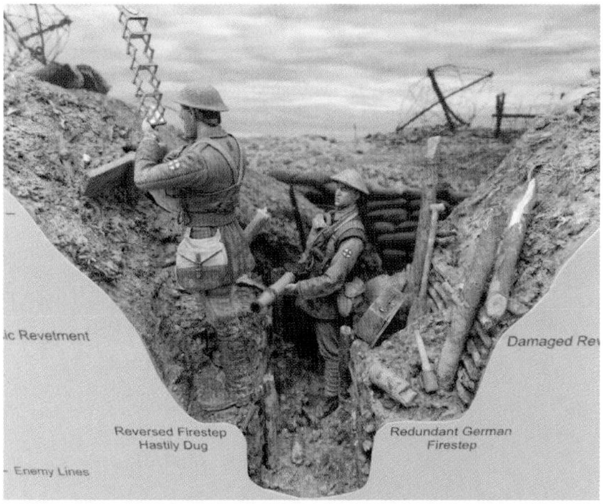

The officer stands on the hastily dug 'reversed' firestep, watching the approaching enemy.

Chapter Eleven

Typical German Trench

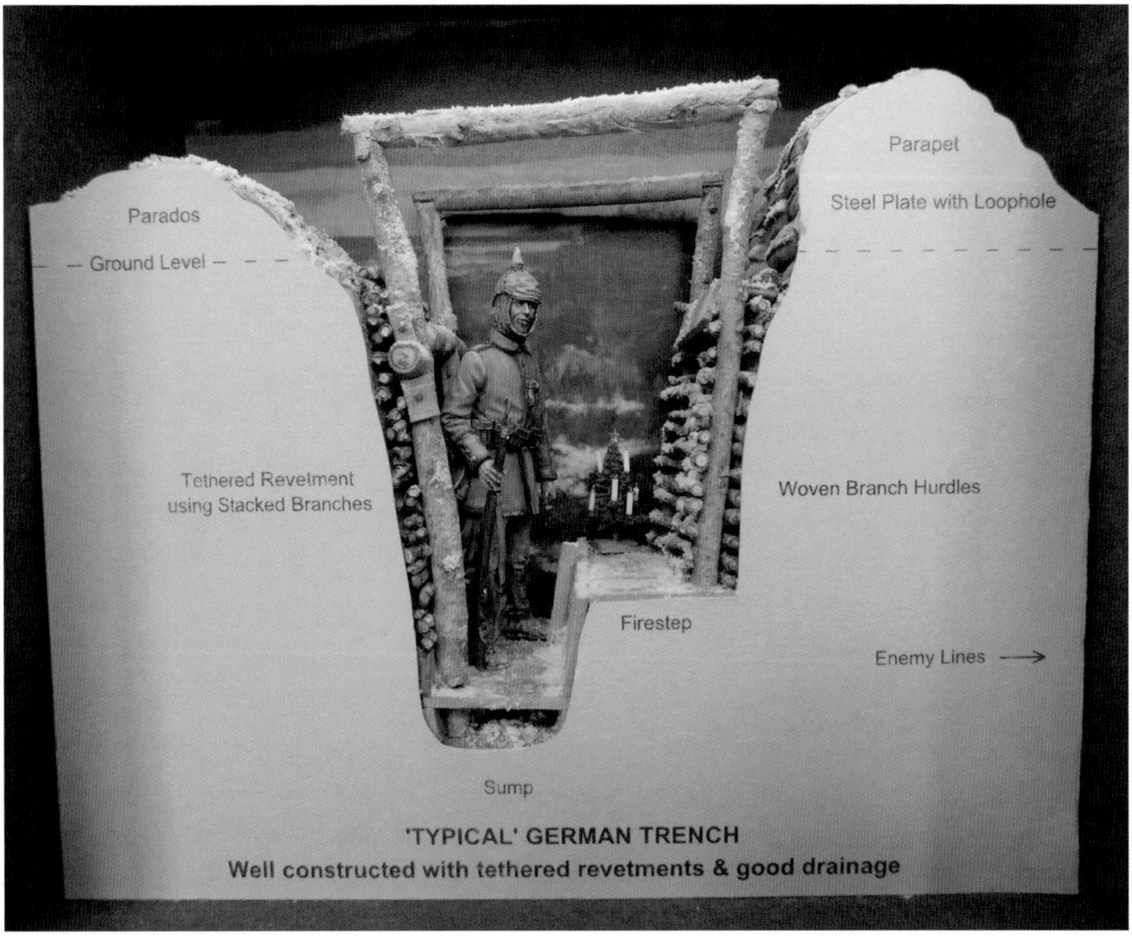

Typical German Trench section in its display box.

The German commanders had a very different attitude towards their trenches than the Allies. They had captured territory on the Western Front at the beginning of the war and then mostly stayed on the defensive, trying to keep hold of the captured land, meaning that they encouraged their troops to build strong, well-built lines of defence with deep dugouts and concrete pillboxes well before the British or French did the same. German trenches were often deeper than those built by the Allies and they used timber and branches much more than the British. They favoured the use of hurdles made of woven branches because they had noticed that branch hurdles could flex back into position after the shock wave had passed, whereas sandbags or corrugated iron revetment would often be destroyed under similar circumstances. Branches could be gathered from nearby, so less materials needed to be transported. The model shows various types of wooden revetment. The parapet wall of this trench has a woven branch hurdle, whereas the back wall is made of piled

Reconstructed German trench at Memorial Museum Passchendaele 1917, Belgium.

Reconstructed German trench at Memorial Museum Passchendaele 1917, Belgium.

Close-up of parados wall revetted with piled branches.

branches, held in place by thicker vertical posts. The base and firestep are lined with sawn timbers with a small drainage sump underneath.

The Germans also liked using metal plates on their parapets, with small loopholes to fire through, usually made of two sheets of steel, spaced apart with a hollow between. Many had an opening cover, operated by a lever on the inside face. The problem with loopholes is that they pinpoint where a soldier will appear, so the Germans would place several loopholes near to each other, to make it less apparent which one was being used. This loophole is firmly held in place by sandbags, but many would be placed in gaps between sandbags on the parapet and could be lowered to give a wider field of fire if necessary.

Another typically German structure was the use of crossbeams over the top of the trench, built at the top of the support posts. The support posts would be held firmly against the soil walls, but it also meant that cover could be placed over these beams, either for shelter or camouflage.

On the parapet lie some stick grenades. The Germans entered the war with a stock of these small bombs, which could be carried by infantrymen for local bombardment. When trench warfare developed, their need became much more apparent. The German stick grenade had a 10-inch wooden handle with an explosive head. A cap at the opposite end was unscrewed to reveal a pull-cord, which would detonate the grenade in either 5.5 seconds or 7 seconds, depending on its type, which was marked on the wooden handle. The British started the war without a suitable equivalent and their first hand-held bomb was complicated and hard to mass-produce. Until the Mills bomb was developed, the British had to make do with crude 'jam tin' bombs, which were explosives packed into old tin cans with a short fuse on top.

The soldier on this section wears an early-war uniform, including leather jackboots and Pickelhaube headwear, under its cloth cover. As the war progressed, the German uniform became simpler as the Allied naval blockade took its grip. Because of shortages, soldiers were issued with boots and puttees rather than leather jackboots. The Pickelhaube was replaced by the *Stahlhelm* 'coal scuttle' steel helmet, far better than the British or French equivalent because it offered good protection to the neck as well as the head.

Reconstructed German trench at Hawthorne Trench, Kent.

The front of the parapet loophole with snow.

Re-enactors of the Infanterie-Regiment 28.
MILITARY ODYSSEY

CREATING BRANCH REVETMENT

I usually take shortcuts when I can, so I looked around for twigs that I could use as small branches for this section. I did not have to look very far as I have three birch trees, which shed long, thin twigs all over my garden. The twigs have buds spaced along their length, but these can be cut off to look as if side branches had been sawn off. Some slightly thicker twigs were chosen for the vertical posts of the parapet hurdle and these were inserted into a jig, made from a scrap of wood. The jig had holes drilled every 20mm for the vertical posts, and then thinner twigs were woven between them. The hurdle was made about 80mm long, so a 50mm area could be selected within its length.

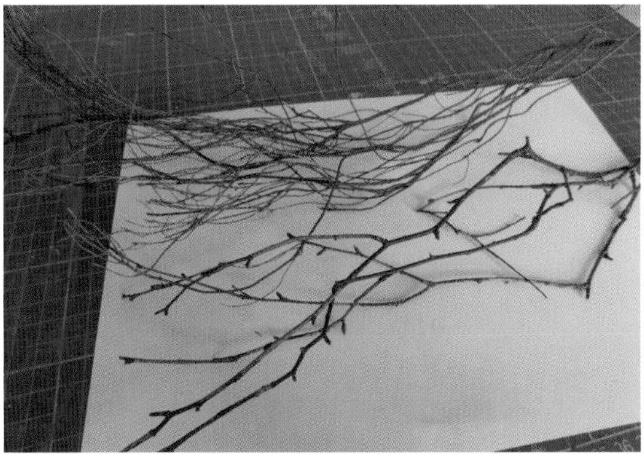

Birch (darker with buds) or heather twigs can be woven into scale hurdles.

As each piece was woven small drops of superglue and PVA were put between the twigs, where they touched and where it would not show. Alternating the direction of each weave, they soon gained strength. Once this hurdle was fully dry, the vertical posts could then be pulled from the jig and the hurdle trimmed to a 50mm width.

The hurdle made from woven birch twigs.

Close-up of the parapet hurdle and loophole.

A balsa capping was made for the hurdle below the loophole, as it would be very uncomfortable to rest your elbows on the hurdle while firing.

Section awaiting paint. The wooden pieces are kept loose until after the groundwork is spray-painted.

The firestep and trench floor were clad with balsa to represent sawn timber and a space was left below the boards for a rainwater sump. You will see from the progress photos that the vertical timbers were replaced to allow overhead cross-beams to be added. The vertical posts were very carefully removed to be replaced with longer ones and rebates sawn into the crossbeams so that the end grain of the vertical posts would be covered from weather damage. Horizontal beams were also made to go between the posts, to stop them flexing sideways on the parados wall. The parapet posts were already secure within the woven hurdle. Rather than painting these twigs, they were given a light dry-brush to help them blend in as scale branches. (Finer hurdles can be woven using heather twigs, and you will find examples of this on the German bunker model.)

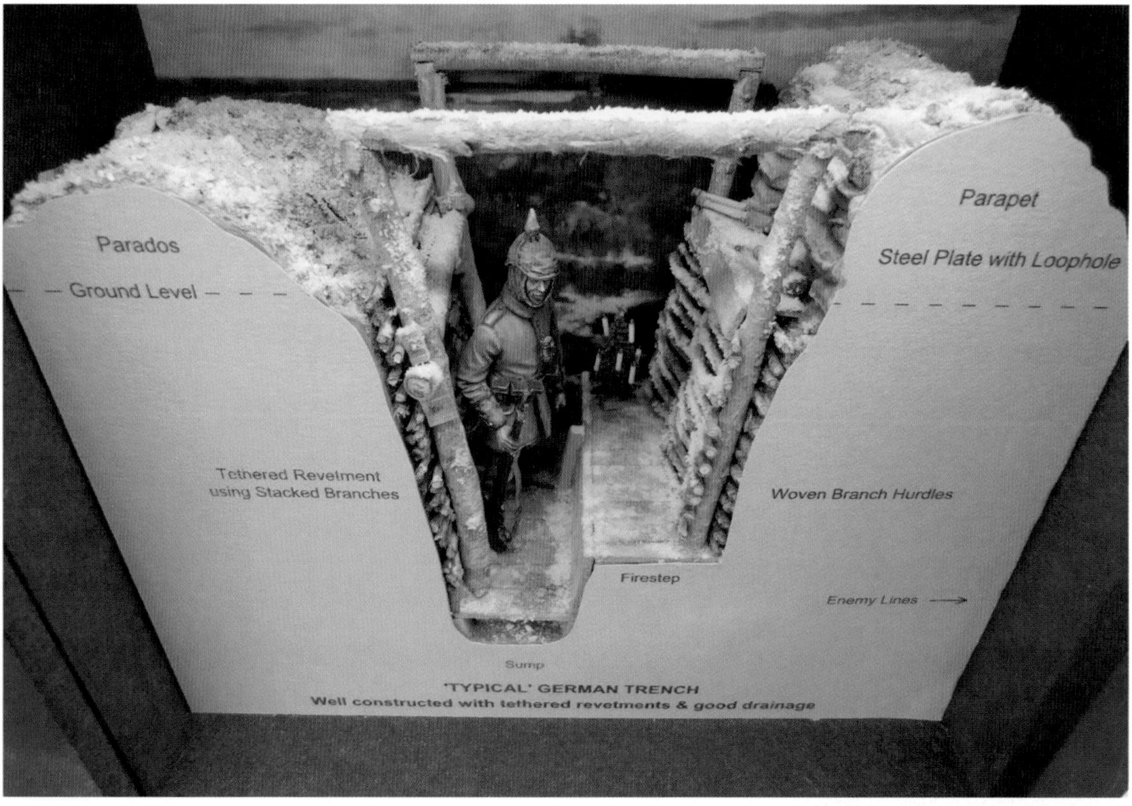

Overhead crossbeams were added and a dusting of snow.

Useful Tip

Glues have differing benefits and you can use more than one at the same time. Superglue will fix something quickly, but is brittle. PVA, on the other hand, will dry slowly but will make a stronger, more flexible, joint in the long term.

CREATING DETAILS

Styrene Branch Hurdles

When making Tommy's War masters, I have to think carefully how something will mould because it cannot have undercuts. Woven branches have many undercuts and are difficult to mould unless the areas behind the weave are filled in. My German base hurdle was built on a polyurethane base, which is a block material that machines easily into the shapes needed. The hurdle was built up on it using half-cylinder styrene strips, which varied between 1mm and 2.5mm. You will see from the progress photos that the vertical posts were placed on first and then horizontal rods woven over them. These had to be cut and sanded with tapering ends, which made it look as if they went behind the vertical posts. Some photos from the war show hurdles whose weaves were in groups rather than purely of alternating branches. This would be easier to mould, as there are fewer undercuts. Once the woven branches were in place, car body filler was added behind each outstanding branch and any gaps between them. The filler was added as it cured and crumbled, so that it would look like crumbling soil. Dry Polyfilla was also used to fill other gaps as it dries slowly and is easier to place. The effect may be judged from the painted diorama of British trench raiders in the Introduction. (For how to make soil using car body filler, *see* Chapter 2.)

Styrene rods that appear to weave. Master under construction for Tommy's War.

Master for Tommy's War German trench. This later war figure wears puttees and boots rather than jackboots.

Useful Tip

When making woven branches with styrene rod, bend it randomly before use because real branches are rarely straight.

Sandbags blended together with Milliput.

Metal Loophole (*Infanterieschild*)

The loophole on this section was made from two rectangles of 1mm styrene. They were double-sided together and two 2mm holes drilled next to each other. They were then filed into one long hole with rounded ends. Once this hole was ready, the two rectangles were separated and spaced with 1mm styrene strip. A 1mm cover was inserted for the loophole and the lever made from pieces of styrene strip.

Sandbags

The sandbags for this section were made before the better method of sculpting with FIMO had been tried (*see* Chapter 4). Resin castings were sanded on their top and bottom surfaces so that they were a little thinner to bed them together well.

Once superglued together, Milliput was pasted between to blend them together. Sandbags were built around the loophole plate and the loophole bridged with a balsa plank.

Snow

After completing the base I decided to add snow to it after my work colleague Craig Hedgecock made a trench diorama with snow on it. Trenches had to be manned all year round, in all weathers. The figure is wearing a balaclava and I painted mittens on his hands. German belt buckles had the inscription 'Gott mit uns' ('God with us'). British troops would tease the Germans by calling out, 'We've got mittens too!'

My snow was added using Deluxe Materials Snowflakes powder, made of fine white granules that have sheen to them. This can be mixed with watered-down PVA glue (50/50) to make slush, or you can paint glue on a surface and apply the flakes. A small Christmas tree (Tannenbaum) was added to the firestep, made from a twisted wire tree, decorated with styrene candles and star.

The parapet with snow and painted figure.

FIGURE

The figure for this section is from the Tommy's War 1914 Christmas Truce set (TW32S02). His flat cap was replaced with a Pickelhaube, which was a Tommy's War spare part, and a Gewehr 98 rifle was from a JMD spare parts set; these are no longer available, but Jon Smith Modellbau now sells German equipment spares. His arm had been reaching out to shake hands, but it was angled down to grip his rifle. A new hand (a Historex spare part) had to be found as the original one was moulded with a British hand attached. Tommy's War now have quite a selection of single German figures.

Basic Guide to Figure Painting

Figure painting is something that I struggle with. Having close friends like Adrian Bay and Mike Butler is intimidating, although they would only give constructive advice if I asked. I leave long gaps between painting figures, which means that I have to relearn during my brief forays into the world of figure painting. My ability frustrates me and I hurry

Converted German figure awaiting paint.

The figure in place, showing the Tommy's War box art behind, from which he was adapted.

towards the finish. Commercial modelmaking has encouraged me to rush to make a profit, so I have to consciously slow myself down and be patient. I regularly use quick techniques like dry-brushing and washes to accentuate detail. A filter wash over dry-brushing will soften its harshness. Even using an Optivisor my painting lacks the precision I desire and my style is much more 'impressionist' than I would prefer, so my work does not allow much magnification. I want to be so much better than I ever achieve and I am much more confident about making things. I will give the very basics on figure painting and leave it to those more qualified than me to tell you how it is done well. I muddle along, getting a reasonable result eventually, but I am not quite sure how I got there!

Painted figure with his 'Tannenbaum' Christmas tree.

Useful Tip

Comparison eats contentment quickly! Do not waste time beating yourself up for not being as good as someone else. Just enjoy what you can do well and aim to be better.

Nowadays nearly everyone uses acrylic paints, which dry fairly quickly and are usually matt. Many use Vallejo paints, but I have a set made by Andrea Miniatures. I usually mix my own lighter and darker tones for shading from the base colour, but these days you can buy many paint sets specially made for the likes of flesh tones or British uniforms.

The most important part of a figure is his head, especially his eyes, and you will need brushes with a good point if you expect to paint fine details like the eyes well. Eyes painted well make an average figure look much better. I do not paint the whites or coloured iris of the eyes on a 1.32 figure, as they are not seen from a distance. Use Burnt Umber darkened with a little black for extreme dark lines. Paint a thin line for his top lashes, which has a sharper incline near the nose, and then add a semicircle centrally, and below this, for the iris. If the eye is too big, you can paint flesh colour under to reduce it, but make sure that the eyes are the same size and point in the same direction. Paint the whole face with a flesh base colour before adding shadows of dark flesh and brown. As always, I try to use very little or no black and white, opting for dark brown and off white. Flesh is best highlighted with a yellowish white on exposed areas like his nose or the top of his cheeks. You have to study faces to get an idea what should be in shadow and what should be highlighted. Practice makes perfect. Where beards grow a small amount of Payne's Grey can be added to simulate stubble. When I am happy with the face I add a wash of Burnt Sienna oil paint, thinned with turpentine, which gives flesh a slight sheen and translucency.

Clothing should be blocked out in its basic colours before tackling smaller details like belts and pouches. Light on a model will affect it differently to full size, so shading has to be emphasized for it to look good. Shade the clothing with darker and lighter shades of the base colour. Surfaces facing upwards should obviously be lighter, and those facing down or in folds should be darker. Split your painting into areas like an arm, or between belts and equipment, which will allow you to blend the paint while it is still damp. The blend between dark and light paint is best made using another soft, damp brush. You need to make sure that you use the same shades throughout for a consistent look over the whole piece of clothing, but dividing it into smaller areas will help with the blending process. You can add dark 'pin wash' with a fine brush into creases or seams, and 'filter washes' are useful to help blend highlights and shadows into the base colour.

Useful Tips

Dark 'pin wash' is applied specifically to flow along a recessed areas to enhance shadow without colouring the surrounding paintwork.

Pin wash with oil paint in white spirit is easier to manage as the pigment in water-based wash can diminish as it dries.

Old brushes that have lost their point can be reserved for stippling and dry-brushing since both of these techniques will damage brushes.

Figures in trenches would usually be splattered with mud, which means that, if painting has not gone well, you can often hide it under some mud. Wet mud is darker, but lighter where it is drier on its edges. Areas of contact like elbows, bottom, knees and boots are the most likely places to be muddy. I usually use Raw Umber for darker 'wet' mud, but mostly use Fawn and Moonstone where it is drier, stippling it onto the clothing with stabbing motions.

Chapter Twelve

German Concrete Bunker

German Concrete Bunker in its display box.

The Germans started using concrete as early as 1915, experimenting with steel rods and pre-casting blocks, which could be fixed together quickly at the front. Many of their structures were built as dugout shelters for troops, but others were purpose-built bunkers for machine guns because the importance of the weapon on the battlefield soon became apparent. They were called bunkers, block houses or 'pill boxes' (due to their similarity in shape to packages in which medical pills were once sold). Because the British and French High Command wanted to win back territory, they were very reluctant to invest time making permanent structures, but the Germans' successful use of concrete, enabling machine guns to dominate an area, forced the Allies to reconsider this and they were eventually making concrete structures of their own.

Many bunkers were built with loophole slots though which a machine gun could be fired, but other shelters had none or just had small viewing windows, and the machine gun would be fired across the roof when the bunker was not being shelled. Bunkers would be positioned with loopholes on the side so that guns could fire obliquely across no man's land, providing support for neighbouring bunkers. This meant attackers had to pass though the field of fire of at least two guns. Their entrance would always be on the back wall, accessed from an entrenched position. The walls facing the enemy were often built of thicker construction (up to 1.5m in thickness). Bunkers could withstand a huge amount of shelling: even direct hits could cause damage rather than destroy them. Some survived near-misses by heavy artillery, which moved the whole structure to settle back on the ground at an odd angle. The shock wave of shells hitting the outer surface would cause sharp shards of concrete to fly around inside, but this was preferable to the danger of living without shelter.

Bunkers would be sited in folds of the ground and camouflaged with turf, rubble or wood to suit their environment and disguise their silhouette. They would be dug into the surrounding ground, giving the structure a low profile, with any loopholes

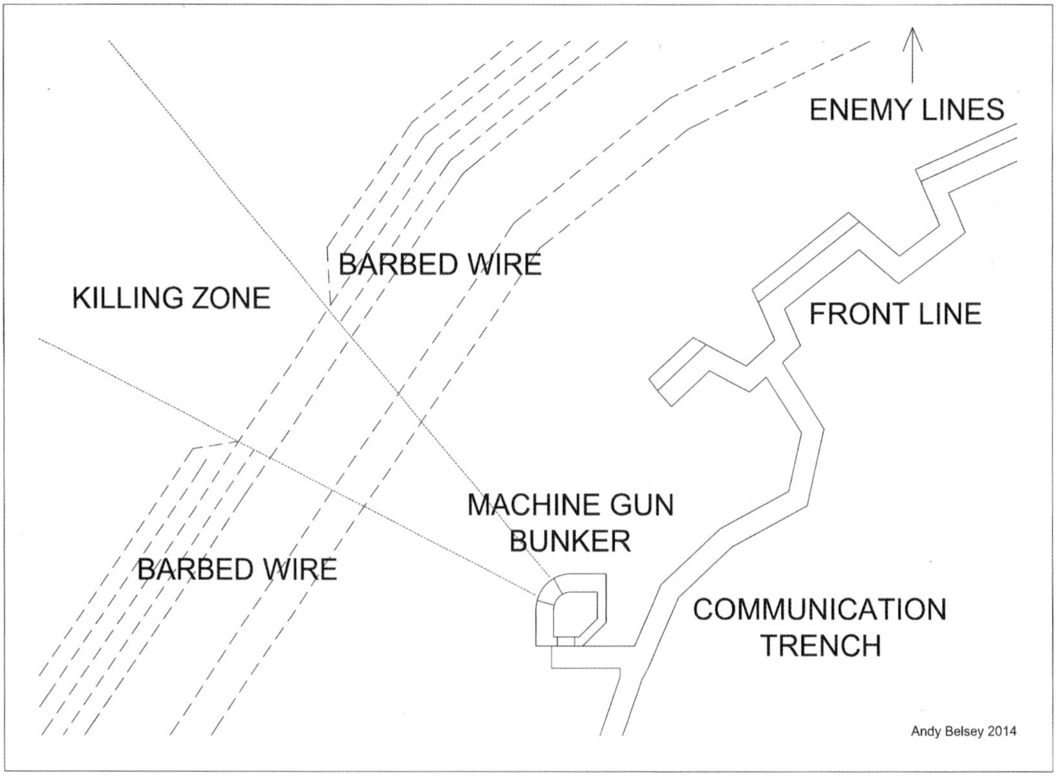

Machine guns would fire obliquely across no man's land and be supported by a neighbouring bunker, so attackers were under fire from more than one gun.

British troops attack a German bunker built into a house. Illustration from Frank A. Mumby, The Great World War: A History, *9 vols (Gresham Publishing Co., 1915–20).* SIMON PARFITT

The bunkers were sunk into the ground and camouflaged to disguise their whereabouts.

being just above ground level. Often they could be so well hidden that they were difficult to locate until you were very close. When troops could get sufficiently close or behind them, weapons like grenades or flamethrowers would be used to clear them. Although they offered good protection, they were not an ideal place to be caught in, especially if a bunker had pinned down an attacking force for a long time. When they were eventually overpowered, no prisoners would be taken.

By 1917 concrete pillboxes had become the cornerstone of German defence. After Passchendaele the British began to take concrete structures more seriously because of the impact they had on a battlefield. When a bunker was captured, it was often a liability, as it now had the entrance and thinner back wall facing forward. The new owners would be forced to blow a doorway in the thicker wall, which was now the back wall, or build a new wall in front of the doorway, making it vulnerable.

This model shows a bunker with an oblique loophole to fire through. Its front wall is twice as thick as the rear wall, which has an entrance leading from a communication trench. It is dug into the surrounding ground, giving it a low profile, and its roof is covered with soil, debris and vegetation as camouflage. The front face has been damaged by shrapnel and small arms fire, revealing some of the steel reinforcing rods. A wicker hurdle has been placed in front to help disguise the concrete structure.

The rear doorway leads into the communication trench.

The raised area inside was created to mount the tripod of an MG 08. When the British began to use the Lewis gun, the Germans experimented in creating their own light machine gun and the result was the MG 08/15, seen here. It was still very heavy but, being mounted on a bipod, reduced much of the weight and the number of crew required to carry it around. It has a drum magazine, allowing one man to carry and fire it. He would have crew supporting him and to carry extra ammunition. The seated private keeps an eye on the battlefield through the loophole, but is in conversation with an NCO, who has just entered the bunker. The private wears a comfortable field cap, but has a helmet ready in case a bombardment starts. Boxes of ammunition are stacked ready nearby.

CREATING THE BUNKER

The shape of this bunker was copied from an original plan found on the internet. It was basically a cube with one curved corner, which has the loophole in it. It was just large enough to house an MG 08 mounted on its tripod or on a wooden sledge, and the area behind the loophole was built up for the tripod to sit on. The gun shown on the model is the MG 08/15, which had a bipod rather than the heavier tripod. There is a second shelf, behind the loophole, for the bipod of this gun to sit on.

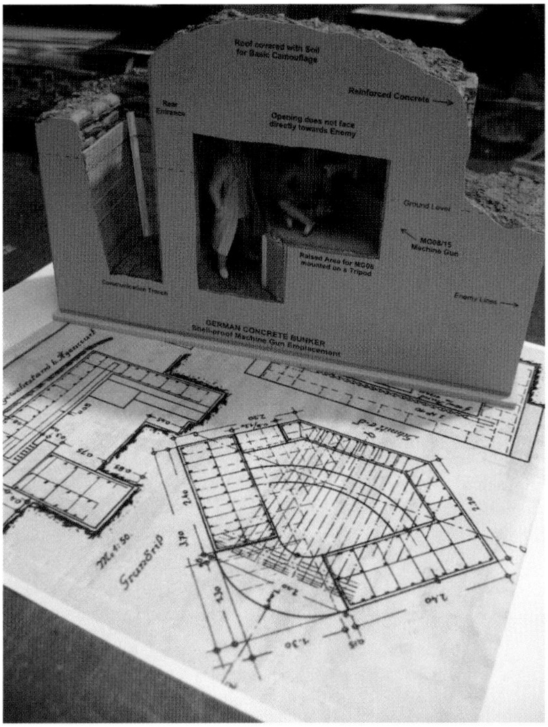

The bunker with plans showing the full shape of this type of bunker.

The main box structure of this section was made from sheet acrylic, but the walls of the bunker are made from high density polyurethane. Sadly this is far too expensive for a hobby modelmaker to buy, as it comes in large sheets, but it is similar to some of the denser balsa foam products that are now available. Polyurethane was chosen because it can be carved or machined to any shape. When you poke a scalpel or chisel into it and flick outwards, it crumbles like masonry.

Damaged concrete and bullet holes were easy to create by carving the plastic with little effort. The walls were made from solid lumps of polyurethane with horizontal groves scribed and wood grain scratched into the walls to represent the wooden shuttering used to pour the wet concrete into. Reinforcement rods, exposed by shelling, were made from 1mm styrene rod, but it would have been easier to bend if they were made from a paper clip or solder. Holes were drilled into the polyurethane and the rods bent and inserted, copying their structure from photos found online.

Lumps of polyurethane make up the sections of concrete in the usual acrylic base. Note that the front wall is twice as thick as the rear wall.

Shell damage is gouged on the front concrete exposing reinforcing rods.

Painting Concrete

Having primed and base-painted the concrete with Moonstone grey cellulose paint, it was given a thin wash of Raw Umber acrylic paint to accentuate the 'wood grain'. Dark pin washes were given to emphasize the seams. Bunkers in the Tyne Cott Cemetery in Belgium have small pebbles in their concrete mixture, so the model's groundwork was masked and the concrete areas speckled with a spray gun. If the air pressure is reduced, a spray gun will spit paint out. You have to experiment with the thickness of paint and amount of air pressure to achieve the size of speckle that you desire. To give the concrete more texture, speckles were sprayed in three colours: very dark grey, mid-brown and off-white. The concrete was dry-brushed and some areas stippled with green and yellow as mould and algae.

German concrete bunker within the Tyne Cott Cemetery, Ypres, Belgium.

The concrete is given speckles of dark grey, brown and off-white.

Groundwork and Trench

The access trench was revetted with balsa and cast sandbags. The angle iron posts were made from 2mm 'L' section styrene and tied with thin electrical wire to represent the tethers, which would be staked into the ground behind. The exposed external trench timbers are grey because they have been weathered more, whereas the internal wood has been sheltered and is more buff yellow. Where the wood has been sitting in moist soil green moss has been added with paint stipples. The sign was made from balsa painted white, with the lettering marked with a fine permanent pen.

The groundwork was made using curing car body filler and painted before adding vegetation. Grass made from carpet underlay was added to the ground in front of the bunker and in areas on the roof (for a description of how to lay grass, *see* Chapter 13). Vegetation would be encouraged on the roof and it has been littered with debris to help blend the structure into its surroundings. I have

Soggy footprints lead into the bunker, which is lit by a small lamp. Note the grey weathered external wood compared to the buff internal wood. The bucket and spade were added to detail a bare corner.

added real dried tall grasses among the shorter grass. The shell-shattered tree was made from a garden twig with its end attacked with end cutters and a scalpel. Shrapnel scars were dug into it with a small chisel. This twig had texture that could be highlighted with gentle dry-brushing. A hurdle was woven in heather twigs to lean against the front wall as camouflage.

Car body filler is added as a soil covering to disguise the bunker and the entrance trench gets some revetment.

The groundwork is added with curing car body filler and further work made to the concrete.

Grass, plants, a hurdle, debris and a tree help to camouflage the bunker.

Useful Tip

Modelmakers are scared to add green plants to their Great War models. Vegetation is not clear in black and white photos and modern coloured images perpetuate the stereotype of pure mud. If you look at contemporary coloured images, however, such as postcards published by the *Daily Mail*, there is plenty of grass in evidence. Weeds grow very quickly, as any gardener knows.

Muddy footprints on the ground were made using Mig's mud (textured) paint. The walls of the footprints were created and then filled with tinted gloss medium. This was given a couple of clear

Water-filled footprints.

coats after for depth. I also added a bucket and spade in the bare corner of the access trench to add some detail there.

Laser-Cut Plants

Among the grass are laser-cut paper nettles, poppies and dandelion leaves, made by the Czech company Fredericus-Rex. The emerald green paper was given a wash of olive green to create a more natural and varied colour. I have converted a pair of Thwaites nail cutters to crimp spines along the paper leaves. They have one sharp jaw that pushes the paper into a piece of half-round tube glued on the second jaw, to bend a spine along each leaf. Flat leaves look very unnatural, so crimping spines and bending leaves at differing angles brings another level of reality for them.

FIGURES

The two figures are made by a company called Kaiser's Army 1914/18, available from Sockel and Bases in Germany (KA54003 and KA54010).

The standing NCO originally had a peaked cap, which was replaced with a head wearing a helmet.

Some alterations have been made to both. The seated gunner's head is turned to look at the standing NCO, who now has a helmeted head made by Jon Smith Modellbau (JSH54). The gunner wears a soft cap for comfort, but has a helmet nearby to grab if a bombardment starts. Neither of them had gasmasks, so they were both

MG 08/15 drum magazine ammunition box. Memorial Museum Passchendaele 1917.

given tins. The gunner sits checking the rounds of a drum magazine on his lap and has also been given a pair of binoculars in order to carefully view the area his gun is covering. (German spare equipment can be purchased from Jon Smith Modellbau.)

MG 08/15 and Ammunition Boxes

Kaiser's Army sell the MG 08/15 (KA54005), which comes with one drum magazine. The ammunition box was copied from one in the Memorial Museum Passchendaele 1917, which could carry two MG 08/15 drum magazines. There would always be a ready supply of ammunition in the bunker, so three boxes were made in balsa gauged by the size of a drum magazine. (Extra castings of the drum magazine were made purely for my own use: I never condone recasting of someone else's work for profit, which is theft!) The metal furniture on the boxes was made in styrene and aluminium foil with wire handles, copied from the original as closely as possible.

Creating balsa ammunition boxes.

USING LEDS

Because the dugout is a little dark internally it has an LED lamp. A hole was drilled into the raised plinth from the base and one of the 'warm' LEDs poked through this. On top of the LED sits a simple lamp made from frosted acrylic, which spreads light up when it is lit from below. The metalwork of the lamp was made in black styrene, which is more opaque than white styrene, so that it would not glow when lit.

There are many types of LED bulb available made for the hobby market (especially for the doll's house world). They are small, easy to use and many can be powered by battery rather than mains. Do not be scared of using them, as they are simple to install. The display boxes have all been lit from above with 12-volt LED strips that have been linked up behind, so that all the models connect to a single transformer, which converts mains power to 12 volts. Because this system was in place, the internal lighting comes from the same power source. LED strip comes in groups of three bulbs, which can be cut and soldered to wires that link them to the transformer.

'Cold' daylight bulbs have been used to light the display boxes, but 'warm' bulbs were always

Painted figures, equipment and interior.

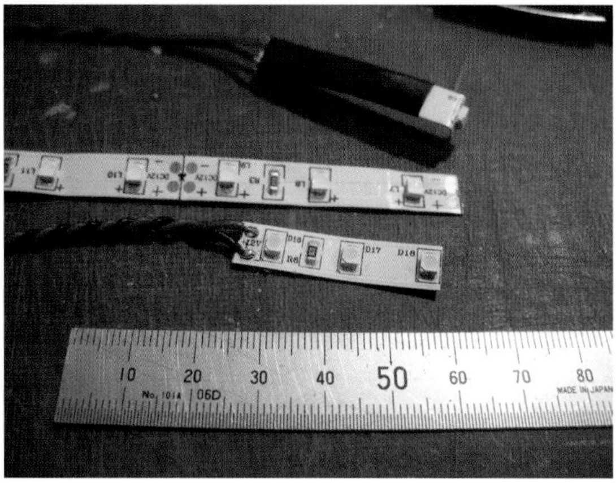

12-volt LED strip lighting, trimmed to use the last bulb. Cool LEDs (lemon) and warm LEDs (golden). Two bulbs can be covered with black insulation tape.

used for internal lighting, giving a more yellow light, much more like internal bulbs or candle-light. Holes were Dremeled through the sides of the sections so that the furthest of the three bulbs could poke through the hole. (You can trim the backing tape back to the end bulb, but you have to keep this type of LED strip in groups of three bulbs or they will not light.) They give off little heat, so the two bulbs that are not wanted can be safely covered with black electrical tape to obscure their light. The furthest bulb can be gently bent at right angles and poked through a wall behind a lamp that you want to light. If you lightly sand clear acrylic, it will spread the light along its surface.

The LED bulb in place, poked through a hole so that the other two are hidden within the base. The lamp sits on top and the light is projected through the diffused acrylic. (Single 12-volt strip bulbs are now available.)

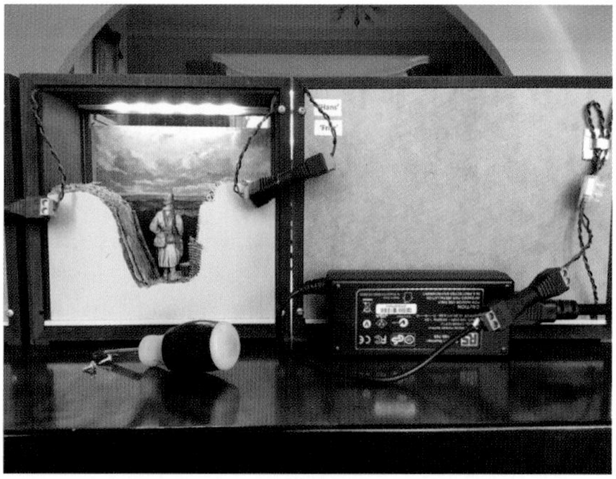

Each display box has a strip of six or nine LEDs in its roof and they can all link together by jack connector plugs to one transformer. Note the extra lead on the right-hand model for internal LEDs, which link into this system.

Chapter Thirteen

British Hospital Tent

'Duty & Devotion': my first project with Mike Butler from New Zealand.

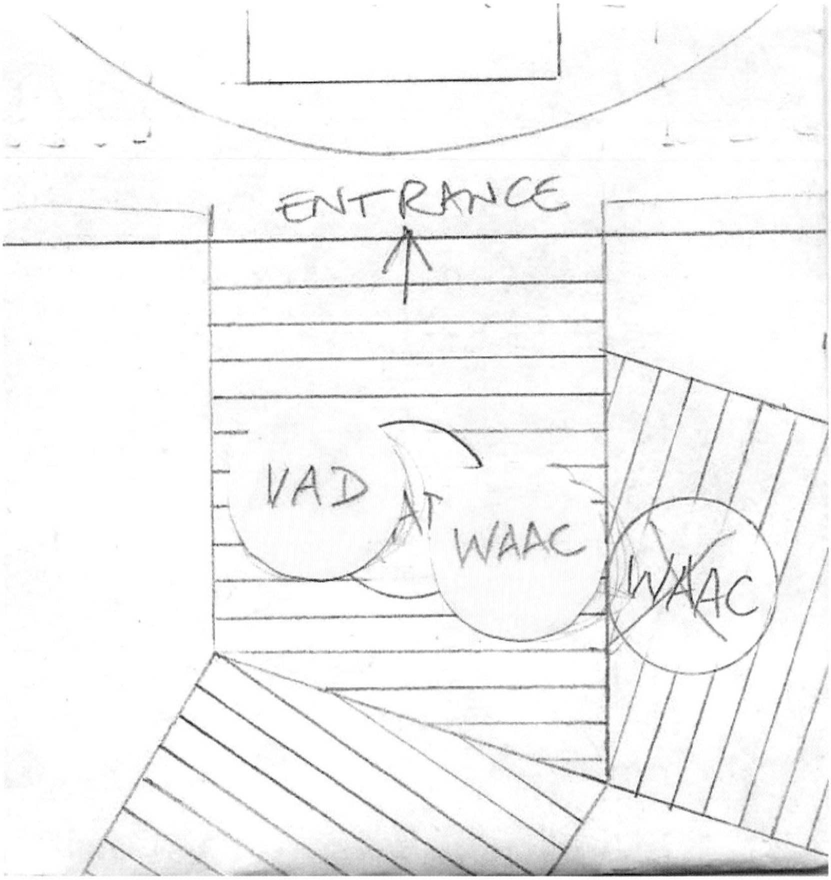

Sketch drawing that helped plan the layout of the diorama.

During the Great War the role of women changed dramatically. The enormity of the conflict demanded that the whole country 'do their bit' and women were asked to do less physically demanding jobs to release more men for active service. Women from all classes volunteered, especially into the medical services, so ladies from privileged backgrounds found themselves doing tasks unforeseen before. Many Field Hospitals were not too distant from the front lines, putting women near to danger. Even when hospitals were clearly marked, stray shells could hit them because they were placed near to the railways that transported the wounded back home. Field Hospitals had to be close enough to the front lines to receive casualties needing urgent surgery as soon as possible, but they also had to be mobile, to move when front lines did, meaning that they were constituted of tents and wooden huts.

This model became my first joint project with Mike Butler, who knew nothing about it until it was completed. He had painted the two beautiful box art figures sculpted by Benoit Cauchies for Tommy's War (TW32A02 and TW32A03). They were sent to Darren Parker-Mead, but neither had a base. In 2017 Mike arranged a holiday with his wife to England that conveniently coincided with Euro Miniature Expo. Travelling from New Zealand and touring around England, however, meant that bringing figures to enter into the competition was out of the question. Darren planned a surprise for him and asked if I could make a base to display both ladies on. We discussed where a Women's Army Auxiliary Corps messenger and nurse might meet, and eventually decided that a Field Hospital tent would make a good backdrop.

PLANNING THE HOSPITAL TENT

Inspiration came from the 2014 BBC series 'The Crimson Field', especially a production photo of a group of nurses walking along a duckboard path towards a hospital tent, which had a Red Cross symbol on its roof to add some colour. The parameters of the model were kept tight to make the figures as the main focus.

The tent would appear more realistic if you could look inside the entrance into the darkness, so I looked for a thin metal that I could bend folds into. Sheet metal like pewter is beautiful to work with, but expensive. A cheaper alternative is pie-tin foil, which comes stamped into a dish shape with webs in it, but these can be burnished out with smooth tools that do not tear or scratch the surface.

Studying photos of tents gives an idea of how canvas folds or sags. Canvas is a heavy material and its shallow creases stem from fixed points, such as tent poles, which radiate out, widening as they get further away and as gravity causes it to sag. The Red Cross emblem would have been made from thinner material, which would therefore have many smaller creases in it.

Creating a Tent with Pie Tin Foil

A rough pencil sketch was made of the tent, from which measurements could be taken. A back and two sides were then cut in 2mm black styrene, giving a firm profile to which the foil could be attached. The roof and two sides of the entrance were cut in foil with a scalpel using a steel rule and engineer's square. The roof piece has a short skirt, which overhangs the side walls to keep out rain and wind. There was only enough space for the bottom tip of the Red Cross symbol, but most people can guess what it is. The arc was marked with engineer's dividers and then the scribe used as a guide for cutting it with a scalpel. The small rectangle of cross was added as a third layer of foil.

Having made all the pieces flat, they were sanded with fine 500 grit sandpaper and seams were marked along their edges, using a pointed but not sharp tool, guided along a steel rule. Folds and creases were then burnished into them. The most useful tool for burnishing is an embossing tool that has different-sized balls at either end. A semi-hard cutting matt is the best surface to work on. The foil curls up either side of where you have burnished, so it has to be bent back again slightly. The smaller ball was used for tighter folds where they bunch together, and the larger ball was better for making the wider creases. The entrance flaps were bent with fingers to create larger and smaller folds, allowing you to see inside the tent. The BBC tent entrance had buttons on one side and strings on the other as fixings to close it. Buttons were made by cutting discs of 1mm styrene rod and cotton was used for the strings. The tent structure under the canvas was indicated by burnishing lines on the inside where the tent poles would sit, but the actual poles were not added as they would never be seen.

Making the tent walls. One flat, waiting to be burnished and folded.

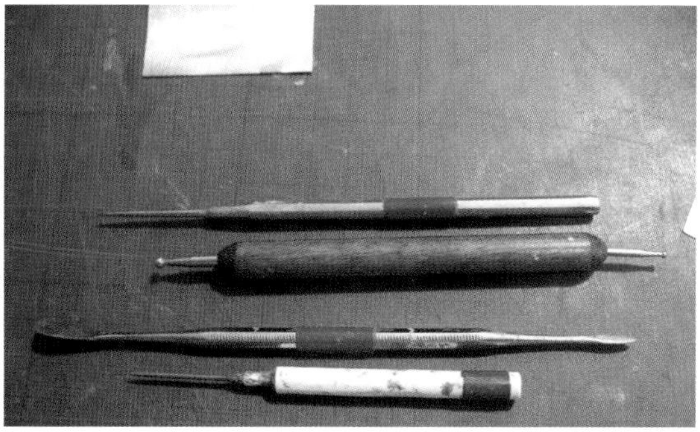

Smooth surfaced burnishing and scribing tools.

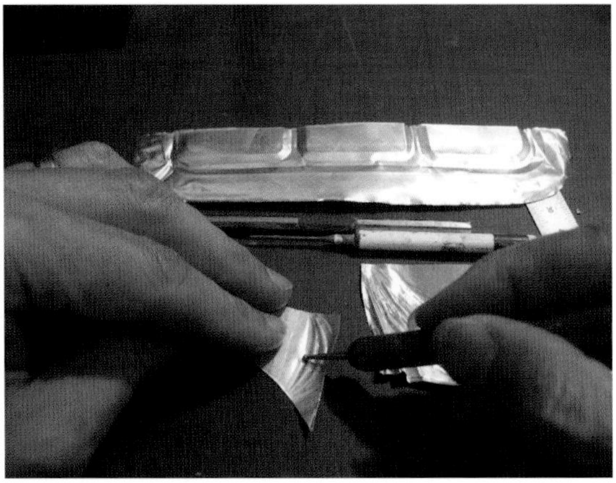

Burnishing sagging folds.

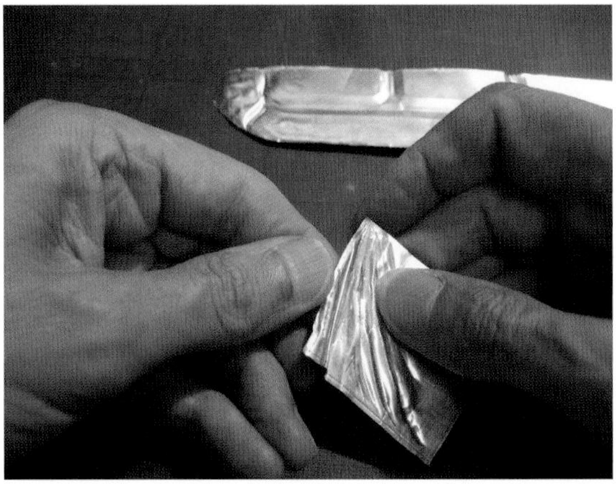

Bending folds with my finger nails.

Balsa Duckboards

The duckboard paths were made with balsa wood using its natural grain highlighted with a thin paint 'wash'. The duckboards in the BBC photo appear to be about 4ft wide, so twice as wide as normal trench boards, and required a central joist as well as those on either side. The main path has a bend in it and is joined by a second path outside the entrance, but the modelled paths were mirrored to give more space on the right because the figure poses interact better with the messenger on the right and slightly in front.

The boards continue inside the tent, covering the only part of the floor that is visible. The joists were fixed with double-sided tape onto a rough

Testing the composition.

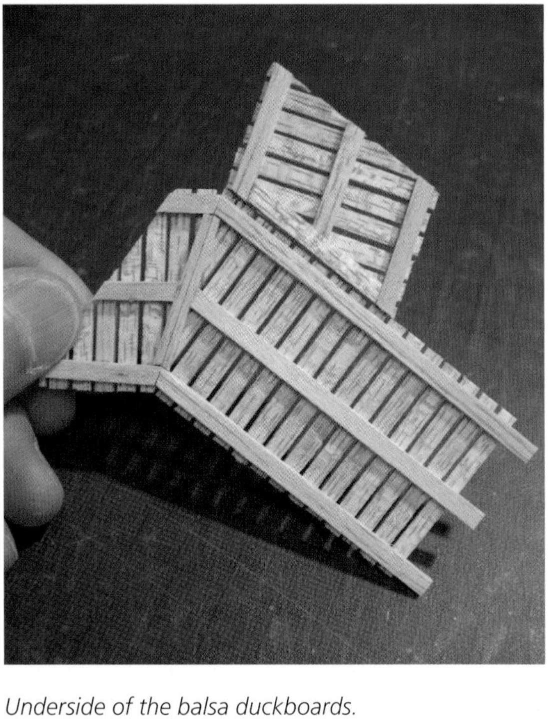

Underside of the balsa duckboards.

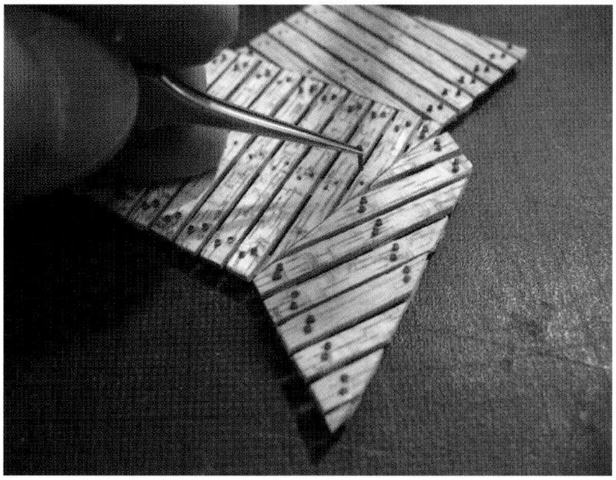

Placing styrene nails into pre-drilled holes.

Nylon tufts placed under the duckboards.

paper plan, while I got the boards ready on top. A number of duckboards of the same length were cut with a guillotine and fixed in place with spots of superglue, leaving small gaps between each board. Where the paths converged it required a little more thought, but balsa is soft and easy to cut with a scalpel. Tapers were cut with a scalpel and sanded a little for fine tuning. Two 1mm holes were drilled into each join, and filled with a styrene 'nail', which sits slightly higher than the boards. As only their heads show, you cannot see whether they get thinner underneath.

Natural wood has differing tones along its length, so three paint washes were applied to the boards – raw umber, then fawn brown and lastly a sandy brown – but in varying amounts in different places. The wash looks quite bright at first but it dulls down as it soaks in and dries overnight. Dark wash was added around the nails, helping to create shadow for them. When the boards were dry, they were dry-brushed with light brown and light grey to vary their colour even more.

Groundwork

Before fixing the boards to the ground, the base was painted dark brown and the positions of the joists were drawn on the groundwork with a pencil. Nylon grass tufts were added in the areas underneath the boards, as you can see between them. After the boards were glued to the groundwork the outer areas were covered with sieved soil, fixed to the base with thinned PVA, which was spread evenly using a brush. (The brush was immediately washed to prevent it going hard.)

Real soil fixed with PVA glue. By working on scrap paper the excess can be tipped back into the storage bag.

Painting the Tent

The foil tent was sprayed with Single Pack Lacquer in order to provide a surface to which cellulose paint would fix. The tent and side walls were then sprayed with black cellulose paint. The tent walls were heavily dry-brushed with a light khaki and the roof with a darker khaki, blending in some shadows and highlights while the paint was wet. I was nervous at having my paintwork so close to

Mike's, and tried to build up some texture to the cloth by stippling with lighter and darker paint to make it look like weathered canvas. It was also stippled with washes, which I think is what Mike calls 'dabbing'. I remember dry-brushing some of the edges, but blended this in with filter wash. Darker, parallel streaks were added over the roof cloth to represent weave. My painting is all a bit of an experiment, which turns out all right in the end, but I am not certain how I get there. The end result is not a blanket colour, but has shading in a number of tones of khaki over its surface. Paint is something I struggle with and I am much more at ease with construction.

The Red Cross disc was sprayed white before hand-painting the shading, masking off the rest of the tent to stay black. The white disc had some light shadows added in a light buff and the seam was painted with Raw Umber. The bottom tip of the Red Cross was painted red and shaded with Raw Umber. Poppy red was used for its highlights. When the tent had been painted, it was fixed to the base, which already had the boards and soil ready to accept it. The folded entrance flaps sat firmly on the boards. When everything was dry the grass was added.

Grass

Grass can be made from various materials such as sisal, which can be cut into short lengths and then painted with green washes of paint. Many like to use ready-made nylon tufts, but these have a sheen that needs to be painted. The grass on this model was made using carpet underlay. I am not sure if this fibrous material is still available, but I found some old carpet underlay in a skip about ten years ago, after reading about using it in a railway modelling book. Short lengths of fibre were cut with scissors and planted tuft by tuft, glued with PVA. Start laying tufts on one side and lay them in rows, working across the area you want to be grassed. Cutting differing lengths gives it a more natural look. Once planted, you can adjust the tufts with tweezers to get them sitting right. The fibres have varied shades of sandy buff and all that was needed was to give some of the grass a wash of olive green acrylic paint. Unpainted fibres were left among the green to make it look like dry grass.

Old fibrous carpet underlay.

Grass made from carpet underlay, laid in small tufts.

The grass is given a partial wash of olive green, leaving some as dry grass.

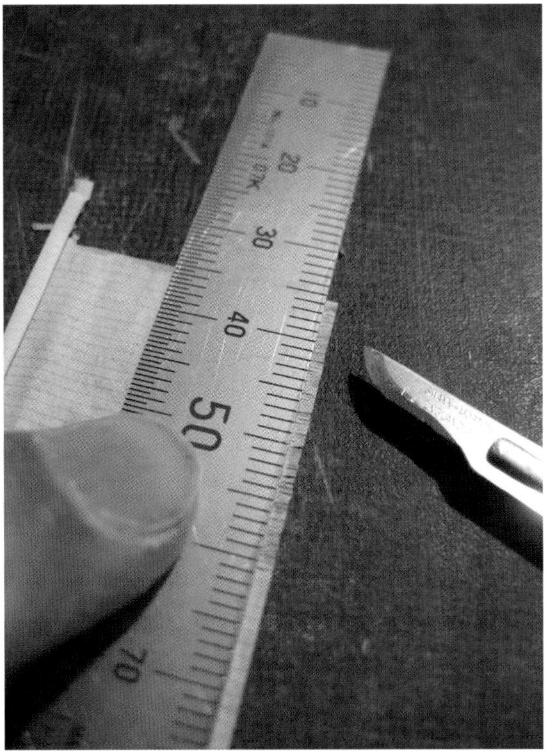

Cutting a dandelion flower comb into the edge of cigarette paper with a no. 10 blade.

Creating Dandelions from Cigarette Paper

The BBC photo had wild flowers among the grass, which was inspiration to add some dandelions as spots of colour among the otherwise drab tones. Laser-cut dandelion leaves, made by Fredericus-Rex, were used, but I did not like the flower heads supplied, so some were made using cigarette paper. Placing a steel rule 1mm parallel to the paper's edge, a series of parallel cuts were made at right angles to the rule every 0.5mm with a no. 10 curved scalpel blade, which was better suited to the task than my usual no. 10a pointed blade. The rule kept all of the cuts to the same length and it was then moved a further 0.5mm to cut a 1.5mm strip of paper comb. Cutting the comb into 20mm lengths and holding an end with fine tweezers, tiny amounts of PVA were put along its spine and it was curled into a spiral. When dry the fine combs that did not have glue on them were

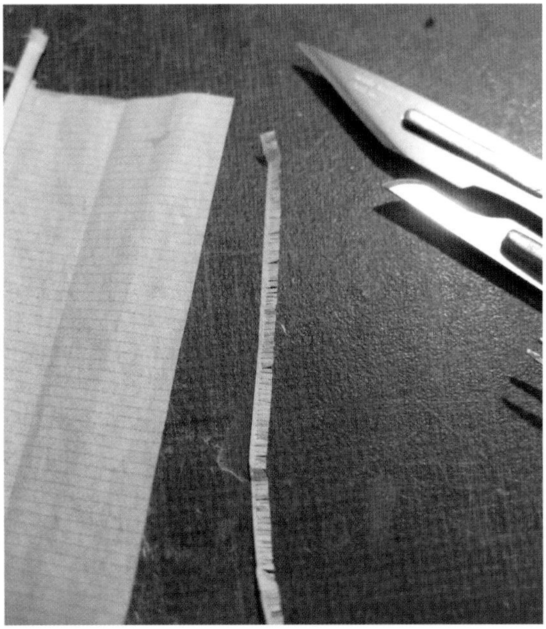

Cutting the paper comb with a no. 10a blade.

Dandelions on my model using Fredericus-Rex laser-cut leaves.

teased out of the paper to make a rounded flower head. Each flower was glued to a short length of wire before painting them golden yellow with an olive green neck and stem.

Spines on the lasered leaves were created by placing half of each leaf into thin-nosed pliers along its length. The exposed half was then burnished to create a fold along the centre of each leaf. Leaves will always look more natural if they are bent at differing angles too, and they were dry-brushed with olive green to vary their colour. (For more details about using laser-cut plants, *see* Chapter 12.)

Tent Ropes

The tent needed guy ropes, which hold the tent poles in place. Cotton is too thin, so fine electric flex was twisted tightly with the aid of an electric drill, while holding on to the other end. This was coated with superglue, in case it unravelled. Each rope runs in an inverted 'V' from the ground to the top of the poles and back down, but one end returns about halfway up again to tensioners. The tensioners were created from styrene strip with two holes drilled in it. The end of the rope was fed through one hole so that the tensioner sat halfway up the rope to join the short length. The end of the short rope was glued into the second hole and knots were made out of cotton, because tying knots in the wire would be impossible. Pulling the tensioner up, so that it sits diagonally on the rope, makes it grip firmly just like the real thing. Ground pegs would be hidden in the long grass, so were omitted. The ropes were sprayed with white cellulose paint and then brush-painted with acrylics. They were given a dark brown wash and dry-brushed with off-white to bring out the rope weave.

Mike names all his figures and has called the nurse 'Vera' and the WAAC messenger 'Gwen'.

Vera and Gwen with their new backdrop.

Note the differing material textures that Mike achieves with paint.

Chapter Fourteen

Great War Artillery

The Great War was essentially an artillery war. The artillery accounted for about 60 per cent of casualties because high explosive, combined with quick-firing guns, made the battlefield so dangerous that troops had to find shelter by digging trenches. This new generation of breech-loaded guns had recoil pistons, which soaked up much of the shock as they fired, meaning that many shells fired in quick succession could be placed on the same target with little re-sighting of the gun. They did not even need a direct view of their target, if forward observers were able to feed back information to report where shells were landing.

Howitzers and trench mortars are designed to lob shells in a high trajectory to land inside a trench that would be sheltered from conventional guns. In addition to explosive shells, millions of shrapnel shells, containing small metal balls, were fired and timed to explode just above the surface, spreading their destruction across a wide area. They were used to destroy barbed wire as well as target troops. Gas shells were developed later in the war, enabling gas to be dropped onto a target area, rather than relying on the wind to carry it towards your enemy.

The Germans began the war with mobile heavy artillery and their successful use shocked the Allies, when Belgian fortresses such as Liège and Namur fell quickly to heavy bombardment. The days of static fortresses were over and thereafter defensive guns needed to be concealed to survive. Heavy artillery was positioned miles behind the front lines, which meant that it was much easier for their shells to fall short and kill their own troops. As a result bombardment of the front lines was left to field artillery and trench mortars.

18pdr gun emplacement: a 1:32 diorama built by Craig Hedgecock, using Tommy's War products.

The British split their artillery into three groups during the Great War. The Royal Horse Artillery in theory supported the cavalry, but in non-mobile trench warfare was merged with the field artillery. The Royal Field Artillery manned lighter guns like the 18-pounder and were positioned closer to the front lines, while the Royal Garrison Artillery manned the heaviest of guns, from 60-pounders (about 2 miles behind the front line) up to huge siege guns on railway carriages, which fired from several miles behind the front lines.

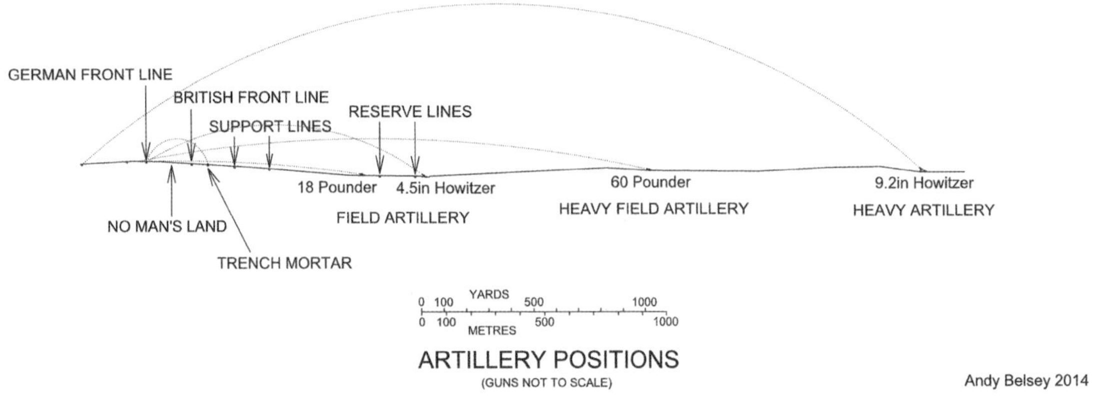

Drawing showing the gun positions.

Shrapnel balls from the Great War.

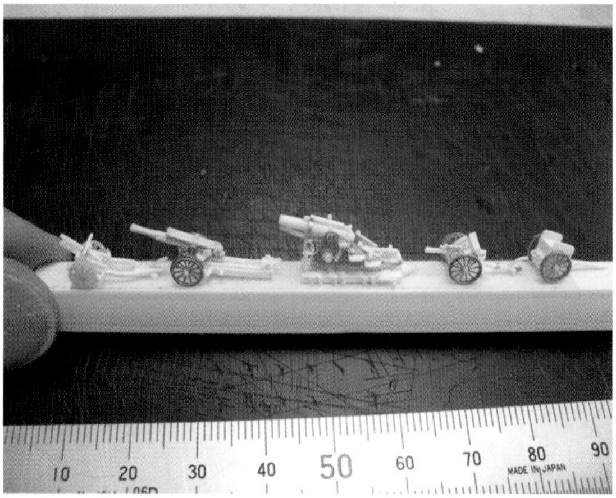

The four guns and limber awaiting paint.

Most of the artillery was transported by teams of horses but, as the war continued and the ground became more devastated, there was a far greater reliance on mechanized tractors or gun carriers, but these too often became bogged down in wet bombarded areas. Gun batteries had to change position regularly, to try to avoid detection, and many hours were spent hauling guns into place. Guns would always have some form of camouflage in the form of netting or foliage to hide them, because counter-battery shelling was common.

MY MICRO-DIORAMAS

The parameters of my 1:285 scale trench model were too small to include artillery, which was positioned at least about 750 yards (685m) behind the front lines. Guns were spaced so far apart that no single model could display various calibres of guns. This required the creation of a series of small dioramas with a 50 × 50mm format. This was chosen as I had used it before to create a series of World War II dioramas, which may be seen on my website. Guns ranging from field artillery to heavy guns were chosen: an 18-pounder, a 4.5in howitzer, a 60-pounder and a 9.2in howitzer.

INSPIRATION

My grandfather was in the Royal Garrison Artillery during the Great War, so I was keen to show his involvement on the battleground. I had already built a 1:285 scale diorama of my grandfather, Ernest Belsey, with his brother Bert, who went to Belgium together in August 1917 to the 108th Heavy Battery of 60-pounders. Although they were put into different gun teams, they saw as much of each other as possible. Ernest had a tough time and expected to die, but although both brothers received small wounds, they both survived the war. The 60-pounder on my micro-diorama is only about 20mm long but is made up of more than eighty pieces. The smallest pieces, which are tiny handles on the crank wheels, are only 0.5mm long and made of 0.25mm styrene. The majority of this model was built using custom-drawn brass etchings and the gun had to be constructed with a pair of tweezers in each hand. I had very good eyesight in 2003 and made it without any magnification aid.

Inspiration was sought from my book collection and the internet for photos of artillery emplacements, to get ideas on how to display the guns. Plans for the 18-pounder and 9.2in howitzer on the Landships II website were printed and reduced to 1:285 scale, but the A4 versions were kept for reference as the smaller versions are so tiny. The Landships II website (www.landships.info) is a source of very helpful information and has articles on many guns of the conflict.

You can buy commercial, war-gaming versions of some of these guns, but none were crisp enough for my liking. I had already built a 60-pounder for my grandfather's diorama and had even made a silicone mould of the barrel, so a new casting was made. That barrel was turned on a watchmaker's lathe, but the recoil pistons were made from several pieces of styrene rod. A 1:32 scale model of a 60-pounder by Scale Link was also used for reference. These days I do not have access to a lathe, which meant that the other gun barrels were made by putting short lengths of styrene rod in the chuck of an electric drill, forming the barrel shapes with needle files and sandpaper as it spun in the drill. The majority of the guns are made from tiny bits of styrene strip, which is available in many sizes. Watchmaker's tweezers are invaluable for fine work as many pieces are too small to work with your fingers.

You will notice in the construction photos that the wheels and crank handles are made from brass etchings, which were produced from CAD drawings. The wheels are made from four layers of

Micro-diorama of my Grandfather Ernest and Great Uncle Bert. The gun is made from about eighty tiny pieces.

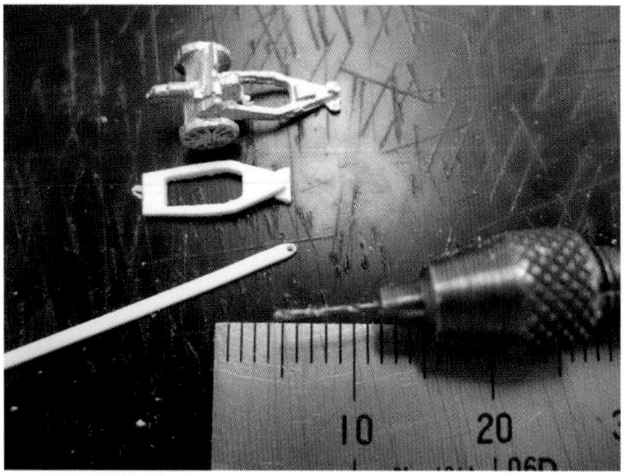

Using a crude wargames 4.5in howitzer to create a refined version.

Creating a 1:285 version with the aid of a 1:32 scale 60-pounder. SCALE LINK

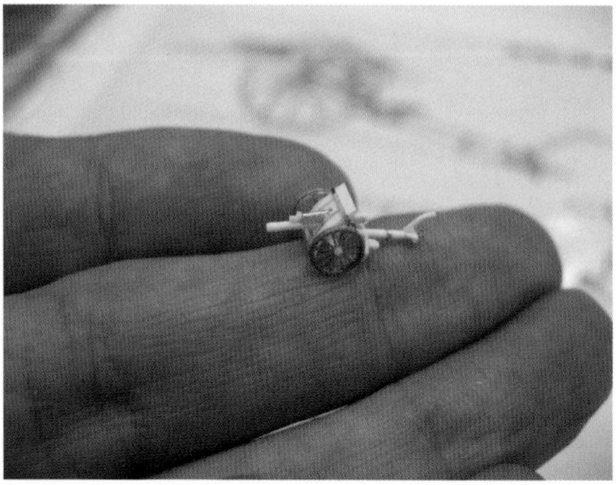

Scratch-built 18-pounder before paint.

etching, stuck together with superglue, to bulk out the rims. The hubs are made from short lengths of styrene rod, with the end sanded into a dome shape. The gun shields were made from 0.25mm sheet styrene, referring to the larger plans and then measuring from the smaller 1:285 scale plans to cut small pieces to the correct length. The other material used on these models is metal foil from scalpel packets, which was cut into fine strips. Fixed with superglue, this will bend and wrap around surfaces to form extra layers of detail.

CREATING MINIATURE GROUNDWORK

Field artillery was usually sited in a shallow pit, with the gun barrel slightly above ground level, helping to hide the position of the battery. All artillery was in danger of counter-battery shelling if it was spotted, so the gunners camouflaged and disguised their batteries under netting or among foliage. This caused a problem as all the detail that I had gone to so much trouble to create would be hidden. I originally intended to display the 18-pounder in a hedgerow, under a wooden shelter, but that would obscure most of it from view. A limber was already made for it, so I decided to put that into the emplacement pit too. Photos usually show a gun with a pile of ammunition next to the gun, but the gun pit was widened to accommodate the limber.

The bases are made from 50 × 50mm blocks of 12mm MDF board with extra layers of 3mm MDF to create contours or the recessed gunpits. The sides of the gunpits were revetted with sandbags, which are resin castings made for the trench model. The MDF bases were coated with car body filler and sprayed with cellulose paint. The floors of the gunpits were lined with wooden boards, made from styrene strips. The boards would prevent the gun wheels from rutting the ground as they recoiled.

The groundwork was given a dark brown wash of acrylic paint to create shadows and to bring out details like the sandbags, whereas the wooden

18pdr in a sunken gun pit to hide its position. Camouflage netting sits nearby if aircraft are spotted.

Layers of 3mm and 12mm MDF create an entrenched emplacement. Resin sandbag castings are added.

Base-coated in Moonstone grey with a filter wash of Raw Umber.

Real finely sieved soil and chalk is added.

boards were picked out with beige 'filter' washes. Soil areas were then coated with PVA glue to fix down finely sieved dust, which had been swept from a garden path. Sieved chalk was also added, as these guns are made to complement the Somme diorama. When the soil was completely dry, fine beige and green foam textures were added for grass, mixed with a little 'static grass' type, nylon flock texture for long grass. This was dry-brushed with ochre and olive green to reduce its sheen.

Useful Tip

When making small scale models, you will need to sieve textures with something like an old tea strainer.

4.5in howitzer in a gun pit, hidden under netting on a wooden frame.

The 4.5in howitzer is in a more standard gunpit, with tapering, sandbagged walls. This gun is under a wooden frame with netting thrown over it to camouflage it from enemy aircraft. This model is difficult to photograph as the view is so narrow, even though the netting is set too tall as a compromise to get some view of the gun.

MINIATURE TREES

The 60-pounder is shown hidden in a row of trees because batteries would hide among foliage whenever possible. The trees were made using brass etchings, which were bulked out with car

60pdr hidden among trees. The gun is about to fire.

Brass etched trunks, which have been bulked out with car body filler.

Scotch Brite-type pan scourer, sprayed grey brown, is added for twigs.

Green and buff foam textures added for grass and foliage.

body filler. I have made trees using the twisted wire method, but I decided not to waste time when I had an easier method. The finer twigs were made from Scotch Brite-type pan scourers, which is best teased out into small clumps and then superglued onto the trunks. The trunks and twigs were spayed grey-brown before spray-glueing fine green foam texture onto them. The trees were planted in the ground by drilling holes into the baseboards and gluing them with PVA.

USEFUL TIP

Always be on the lookout for materials like Scotch Brite kitchen scourers, which can be used for twigs on models.

Always leave gaps between the clumps of tree foliage to avoid them looking like lollipops.

ADDING DETAILS

The 9.2in howitzer is shown sheltered behind a low ridge. Being far less portable, due to their weight, heavy guns like this could not be evacuated if the front lines were taken and so were deployed several miles behind the front. Heavy artillery was used to target enemy strongpoints, communication and supply centres away from the front lines in case shells fell short. Trench planners would often hide trenches just over a rise in the ground because it created a blind spot from standard artillery, but the high trajectory of howitzers and mortars enabled them to reach deep or hidden spots.

The dioramas come to life with the clutter that surrounds the guns and are given scale by the human figures. The figures are really World War II British artillery crew, made by GHQ. Some have been painted with their jackets on, some in shirts with braces hanging down and a few

9.2in howitzer shielded behind a crest. Figures in the foreground prime shells, another pair carry a shell on a cradle, while others get ready to fire the gun.

Adding styrene shells to the 60pdr diorama.

with bare chests. Around the guns you will spot shells waiting for priming, spent shell cases and an assortment of boxes and tools made from small pieces of styrene. Several hours were spent making shells by sanding points on styrene rod, before cutting a shell to length. Painting at this scale demands a steady hand and good eyesight, but having reached my fifties my eyes are faltering. It was making these models that made me accept that I had to invest in magnification and I now use an Optivisor.

The dioramas are now displayed boxed together and lit by LEDs, like the section models. The dioramas are housed within a location drawing that shows where they were sited in comparison with the front lines.

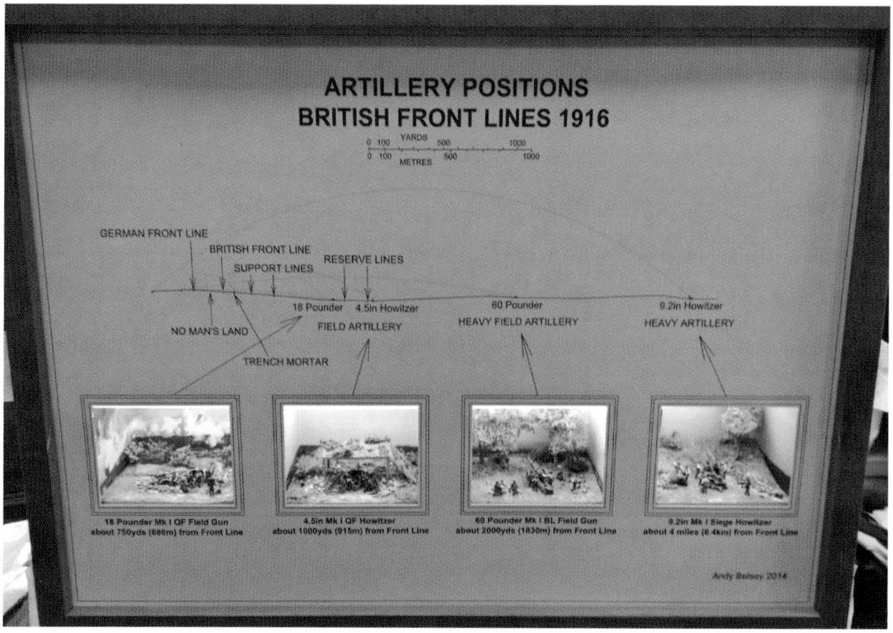

Models displayed to show how far behind the front lines guns were positioned. Note how the howitzers and mortars lob their shell high to land in hollows.

Chapter Fifteen

Visiting Trenches Today

It is one thing to look at photographs of trenches, but it is a very different experience to stand inside one. You may never understand the mortal fear that soldiers of the Great War endured daily, but you will appreciate some of the claustrophobia, confusion and inconvenience that they cause. Below are a few trenches that I have visited for the experience and would recommend that you do the same.

Reconstructed British trench in chalk with mainly sandbag revetment. Hawthorne Trench, Kent.

Sandbags, corrugated iron and duckboards. Grenades would be stored behind the hanging cloth. Hawthorne Trench, Kent.

In the UK you can visit and enter reconstructed trenches in Elham, near Folkestone, Kent. Hawthorne Trench was the brainchild of Toby Dingle, who dug trenches of his own after visiting the battlefields of Belgium and France with his school. His father Richard owns a farm and

Communication trench with A-frames leading to a small elephant shelter. Hawthorne Trench, Kent.

Reconstructed dugout entrance. Note the rolled-up gas curtain. Hawthorne Trench, Kent.

Reconstructed German trench with timber revetment and overhead beams. Hawthorne Trench, Kent.

gave Toby permission to excavate 150 tons of soil and chalk to create replica trenches in a corner of their land. They were joined by historian Andy Robertshaw, who previously had trenches in a plot of land next to his house in Surrey. (His '24Hr Trench' is no longer there, sadly, but photos may be found both in this book and his own publications.) Hawthorne Trench holds open days when Toby will take you on a tour, sharing his wealth of knowledge about the Great War. There is a German trench, as well as extensive British trenches, including a Field Aid Post, small shelter and latrine. Dug into chalk, these trenches recreate what trenches of the Somme region would have looked like.

The best reconstructed trenches in Belgium are at the Memorial Museum Passchendaele 1917. After a tour of the museum, you go downstairs to an extensive, late war, British underground dugout and then into trenches outside. There are German and British

Reconstructed German trench with timber revetment. Memorial Museum Passschendaele 1917.

Reconstructed British trench with A-frames, sandbags, chicken wire and timber revetment. Memorial Museum Passchendaele 1917.

Reconstructed German trench with wicker hurdles and overhead beams. Memorial Museum Passchendaele 1917.

trenches, built in varying styles with shelters in both parts. It is an excellent museum, concentrating on the Third Battle of Ypres in 1917, and the trenches give an extra dimension to your visit there.

Also in Belgium, near Ypres, are original trenches that have been restored. Yorkshire Trench is a section of British trenches rediscovered and restored with modern revetment. They are in the middle of an industrial park and a little difficult to find, but worth the effort to search out.

Sanctuary Wood Museum (Hill 62) has the remains of British trenches surrounded by original shell craters. When the farmer reclaimed his land after the war, he left this area untouched. As the centenaries of the war approached, the trenches were revetted with old pieces of corrugated iron to give an idea of what they would have looked like. The museum has a large collection of war relics, including a large number of stereoscopic photographs of war scenes (some quite graphic).

Yorkshire Trench: rediscovered Great War trench near Ypres, Belgium.

Corrugated iron revetment at Sanctuary Wood, near Ypres, Belgium.

Preserved Great War trenches at Sanctuary Wood, near Ypres, Belgium.

Deep dugout entrance (not open to the public) at Yorkshire Trench, near Ypres, Belgium.

Chapter Sixteen

Finding Inspiration and Encouragement

It is to be hoped you have found this book helpful and learnt something from it. No book can cover everything and these models are obviously not conclusive or perfect. My intention has been to help others understand Great War trenches, which became an awful necessity in a desperate war. War causes many more problems than it solves and eventually the enemies have to negotiate. We should look at history and learn from it, not repeat the same mistakes, taking heed of Albert Schweitzer's words, 'The soldiers' graves are the greatest preachers of peace'.

Neuville-St Vaast German Cemetery, France: 45,000 buried (four men to each cross, with German Jews among them).

Making models for your own pleasure is a great thing, but I am convinced that they are best enjoyed with friends. I grew up with Adrian Bay, who became well known for his models, long before I did. We have been encouraging and helping each other for nearly fifty years now. Working professionally as an architectural modelmaker can sap your enthusiasm, but I have a work colleague, Craig Hedgecock, who shares my passion for military modelling in our spare time. I have enticed Craig away from World War II Nazis to my world of the Great War and he makes excellent dioramas of his own. We advise each other how to make better models.

La Targette Cemetery, Arras: 640 British (foreground) and 11,000 French war graves.

There are many local military modelmaking groups where you can find help and advice about how to improve your work. If there is nobody nearby, the internet offers a different type of community, connecting you with those who share your specialist interests. There are forums catering for those of us who get pleasure from

William Coltman VC (RAMC), 1:30 scratch-built figure by Adrian Bay.

'A Close Shave' by Craig Hedgecock. Tommy's War figures with a scratch-built bunker and scenery.

British dugout entrance with a 1:32 Tommy's War figure by Craig Hedgecock, on a diorama base also created by Craig.

German dugout by Craig Hedgecock. Tommy's War figure with scratch-built revetment.

creating models and you can make friends with someone anywhere in the world. You may be surprised that I have always struggled with self-confidence, but I am very glad that I plucked up the courage to post photos of my work on a forum in 2013, because it has ultimately led to this book and my work getting worldwide attention. These days I blog on Scale Models Forum and Planet Figure.

Scale Models Forum (www.scale-models.co.uk) is a small but friendly community of modellers of varying ability. Its greatest asset is that the 'experts' are not arrogant, so you will find encouragement and help. The site is not particularly competitive, being a place where friends enjoy a hobby together without fear of ridicule. I receive advice and encouragement from fellow modellers and I too have been able to help others. Having friends view the progress of your work allows them the opportunity to spot mistakes or offer tips about how it could be improved.

A site specializing in figure work is Planet Figure (www.planetfigure.com), where you will find some of the best figure modellers from around the world, such as Mike Butler in New Zealand. I have received more constructive criticism on this site, but not abuse, because forums have moderators who guard against maliciousness.

There is less safeguarding on Facebook, but it does have many specialist groups including the WW1 Modellers International Group and Tommy's War Modellers Group, which I have joined.

Model shows give you a chance to meet with friends and enter competitions, if that is what you like to do. Comparison eats up contentment and competing brings stress, so I concentrate on making models just for the pleasure it can bring.

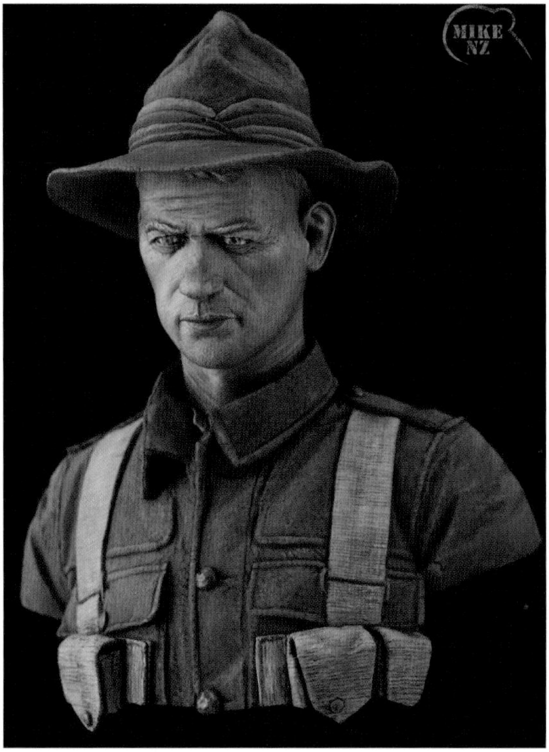

'Vic Nicholson, Wellington Infantry Battalion' by Mike Butler. Conversion from a 1:10 Tommy's War bust.

You can see more of my work, and also more of Craig's models, on my website (https://andybelseymodels.wixsite.com). This may have helped to bring my work worldwide attention, but I am always aware of faults in my handiwork. I have tried, to the best of my ability, to write this book simply and intelligibly, passing on what I have learnt while making these models.

Appendix I

Trench Glossary

A-frame	Wooden frame designed to raise the duckboard walkway above wet areas, allowing rainwater to drain into the space below.
Berm	Small shelf left at ground level between the rear wall and parados soil pile. Soil would be less likely to gravitate back into the trench.
Blighty	Hindustani word used by the British to refer to Britain. It was also used in connection with a wound that was serious enough to warrant you being transported back to Britain.
Breastwork	Trench wall, built above ground level because the ground was liable to flood.
Bunker	A shellproof shelter, often made of concrete.
Chat	A louse (blood-sucking parasite). Soldiers would have informal conversations while trying to remove lice from their clothing.
Chlorine gas	The first type of gas was released from canisters and carried across no man's land by the wind. Introduced in April 1915, it damaged the eyes, nose, throat and lungs.
Communication trench	A winding trench passageway, built at 90 degrees to the front line, which enabled men to pass between the trench lines unobserved by the enemy.
Crater	Hollow in the ground caused by shelling or mining.
Duckboard	Wooden walkway that enabled troops to walk over wet, soggy ground.
Dugout	Underground shelter used as a safer living space, medical centre or office.
Elephant shelter	Small shelter built using 'elephant iron' – curved corrugated iron sheet.
Enfilade	Gunfire from the side, along the length of the trench.
Fascine	A tightly bound bundle of brushwood or sticks. Small fascines were used as revetment, whereas larger fascines were carried by tanks to fill up a trench, so that it could pass over.
Firebay	A short section of trench with a traverse at both ends. It had a raised firestep, from which troops could defend the position.
Firestep	Raised platform, on which troops could stand to fire over the parapet at their enemy.
Front line	Trench closest to the enemy.
Funk hole	A small hollow dug into the side wall of a trench as a basic shelter.
Gabion	Wicker, bottomless basket, filled with soil and used as revetment.
Iron ration	Emergency quota of food carried by British troops, consisting of corned beef, tea, sugar and hard biscuit.

Knife rest	Obstacle made of barbed wire wrapped around a wooden frame. It would be kept on the parapet, but could be pulled quickly into the trench, to give vital moments to escape.
Latrine	Toilet. Usually just a basic hole dug into the ground with simple seating over it.
Listening post	Usually a shell hole in no man's land, nearer to the enemy, from which troops could gain information about enemy movements.
Mustard gas (Dichlorethyl sulphide)	A volatile, corrosive poison gas, first used in 1917. It attacked mucous membranes, lung tissue, eyes and skin, and was much more problematic than previous gases as it remains active for several weeks.
No man's land	The unoccupied area between opposing forces' trench lines.
Over the top	Climbing over the parapet to attack the enemy.
Parados	Soil piled behind a trench, giving extra shelter from shells. If it was built higher than the parapet, it would also partially hide the silhouette of troops exposing their heads.
Parapet	Soil piled in front of a trench as extra protection from gunfire or shelling.
Phosgene gas	The second type of poison gas, more deadly than chlorine, introduced late in 1915.
Pillbox	A bunker or blockhouse, often used as a machine gun post.
Reserve lines	Trenches dug slightly further back from the front and support lines.
Revetment	Support given to trench walls, made from numerous materials, but usually sandbags, timber, corrugated iron or woven branches.
Russian sap	Shallow tunnel dug just under the surface from the front line towards the enemy.
Sap	A shallow trench dug from the front line into no man's land as a forward outpost.
Shell splinter	Small piece of shell casing, which would be red hot at the moment of explosion.
Shrapnel	Small metal balls sent in a hollow shell that would explode above their target to spread the balls in a wide area.
Stand to	At dawn and at nightfall troops would mount the firestep with fixed bayonets, as this was the most likely time of an enemy attack.
Sump	Drainage ditch, which could be a drain under a duckboard passageway or a shell hole designated for dumping water and waste into.
Support trench	Secondary line of defence, close to the front line.
Traverse	A buttress of soil built between two firebays as protection from shellfire or enfilade.
Trench foot	Fungal infection caused by continued exposure to damp. It was extremely painful, could lead to gangrene and even amputation.
Whizz-bang	Light calibre field artillery shell, which exploded quickly after being fired.
Zero Hour	Start time of a military operation.

Appendix II

Useful Measurements at 1:32 Scale

1:1 to 1:32 Factor = × 0.0313
(1m or 1000mm × 0.0313 = 31.3mm @ 1:32 scale)

Actual size	Scale size	Actual size	Scale size
1ft (30.45cm)	9.6mm	1in (2.54cm)	0.79mm
2ft (60.96cm)	19.1mm	2in (5.08cm)	1.6mm
3ft (90cm)	28.7mm	3in (7.62cm)	2.4mm
4ft (121cm)	38.2mm	4in (10.16cm)	3.2mm
6ft (182.8cm)	57.24mm	6in (15.24cm)	4.78mm

Corrugated iron sheet

2ft 9in widths	26.2mm
6ft	57.24mm
7ft	66.84mm
9ft	86mm

	Actual size	Scale size
Sandbag (including neck)	33 × 14in (840 × 360mm)	26.3 × 11.3mm
Sandbag filled (high)	6–7in (150–180mm)	4.7–5.6mm
Offset duckboards	8ft × 18in × 4.2in (2.44m × 460mm × 107mm)	76.4 × 14.4 × 3.4mm
Tapered duckboards	6ft 6in × 18in × 4.2in (1.97m × 460mm × 107mm)	62 × 15 × 3.4mm

(Duckboards could vary greatly in size. These measurements are taken from original examples.)

	Actual size	Scale size
'Flimsies' petrol/water cans	10 × 6 × 11in high	8 × 5 × 9mm high

(Height is for the main body of can, excluding handle or spout.)

Screw pickets	5ft 7in (with 3 or 4 loops)	53mm
	3ft 9in (with 1 or 2 loops)	36mm
	2ft 1in (with 1 or 2 loops)	20mm

GS spade	3ft 2in	30.3mm
Shovel	3ft 1in	29.5mm
Pickaxe	3ft	28.7mm

SRD rum jar (height × diameter)	13.5 × 7in (343 × 180mm)	10.7 × 5.6mm

INDEX